Adam Meggido

Adam Meggido is a writer, director, performer and composer.

He studied Drama and Theatre Arts at Birmingham University and gained a postgraduate diploma in acting from the Webber Douglas Academy, although he cites his years with Claude Chagrin and Ken Campbell as the most important parts of his training.

Adam is the co-creator and director of *Showstopper! The Improvised Musical*, which won the 2016 Olivier Award for Best Entertainment and Family. *Showstopper!* has also enjoyed a BBC Radio 4 series, twelve sell-out years to date at the Edinburgh Festival Fringe, numerous UK tours, and performances all over the world.

He created and directs the annual *London Fifty-Hour Improvathon* and holds the (unofficial) world record for directing continuous longform improvisation (55 hours in Toronto, December 2013). Other projects in improvisation include *The School of Night* (Shakespeare's Globe, Royal National Theatre, Royal Court Theatre), *Rhapsodes* and *The Society of Strange* (Theatre503, Wilton's Music Hall, Edinburgh Festival Fringe, and performances in Norway, Italy and Canada). He also co-created, and performed in, eight online improvisations with ventriloquist and filmmaker Nina Conti, entitled *Nina Conti: In Therapy.*

As a theatre director his credits include *Peter Pan Goes Wrong* (nominated for a Best New Comedy Olivier Award), and *Magic Goes Wrong.* He was consultant director on *Mischief Movie Night* (also Olivier-nominated for Best New Comedy) and *Austentatious: An Improvised Jane Austen Novel* (Chortle Comedy Award winners).

His musical *Burlesque* won four Off-West End Theatre Awards including Best New Musical 2012. He also co-composed music and wrote lyrics for *The Tailor Made Man* (Arts Theatre 2013) and is the author of twelve plays.

Adam is an associate director of the National Youth Theatre of Great Britain and was the Head of Foundation at LAMDA 2007–16 where he has been teaching since 2004.

@adammeggido

IMPROV BEYOND RULES

A Practical Guide to Narrative Improvisation

Adam Meggido

Foreword by Mischief Theatre

NICK HERN BOOKS
London
www.nickhernbooks.co.uk

A Nick Hern Book

Improv Beyond Rules
first published in Great Britain in 2019
by Nick Hern Books Limited
The Glasshouse, 49a Goldhawk Road, London W12 8QP

Designed and typeset by Nick Hern Books
Printed and bound in the UK by
Ashford Colour Press, Gosport, Hampshire

A CIP catalogue record for this book is available
from the British Library

ISBN 978 1 84842 731 0

To all my students
– thanks for the education

Contents

The most vulgar ruffians and mountebanks get it into their heads that they can draw crowds and entertain them with words, and like so many bumptious Hercules in golden chains they try to perform improvised plays in public squares, mangling the *soggetti*, speaking off the point, gesturing like lunatics and, what's worse, indulging in a thousand scurrilities and obscenities, in order to extract a sordid income from the purses of the spectators.

From *Dell'arte rappresentativa, premeditate ed all'improvviso* (*The Art of Staging Plays, Premeditated and Improvised*), 'A Treatise on Acting from Memory and by Improvisation' by Andrea Perrucci, the Neapolitan, 1699

Foreword
Henry Lewis, Artistic Director, Mischief Theatre

'Don't make rules, make principles,' Adam always told us in his improv classes. It's a fantastic ethos not just for improvisation but for theatre-makers and storytellers of all kinds. Rules box you in; principles free you and, in my opinion, it's impossible to create anything that's really original unless you look *beyond* the rules.

I first met Adam Meggido, the extremely wise writer of this insightful book, back in 2008. It was my first day on the One-Year Foundation Course at LAMDA (London Academy of Music & Dramatic Art). Adam was the head of the course and took our improvisation classes; classes which immediately became my favourite part of the excellent theatrical training LAMDA has to offer. My twenty-nine classmates and I sat on the scuffed, beige dance matting at the beginning of an awesome journey.

Adam isn't just an excellent improviser, he's also an excellent teacher of improvisation. Many people who are truly brilliant in their field lack the skill of being able to pass on their genius, and of course there are many great teachers who communicate theory very well, but Adam is a rare combination of both. In his classes, as he does in this book, he transforms the seemingly impossible into something exceptionally practical with his trademark patience, charm and clarity – and from the first session our year group fell in love. How wonderful it felt to be able to walk into class at 10 in the morning and leave an hour-and-a-half later having created two-dozen characters, ten new scenes, five songs and a love story, all while laughing more than we ever had in our lives. In the all-consuming drama-school bio-dome of Shakespearian text, emotional memory and Alexander Technique, improv was an oasis of fun and play – it has informed my career in huge ways. Mischief Theatre may well have never existed without it.

A few weeks into our training, Adam announced that he and his improv gang were presenting a show at The Wheatsheaf, a pub in Fitzrovia. It was an improvised musical he said, with live music and off-the-cuff songs. We all bought tickets immediately and we had the time of our lives watching *Only the Dead Can Dance*. The audience loved every minute, seeing ideas they had just invented off the top of their heads being transformed into live songs and action just moments later. It was hysterically funny, electrically exciting, and as live as live can be. This early iteration of course went on to become *Showstopper! The Improvised Musical,* Adam's brainchild, and probably the most successful live improv show in the world today.

My theatre company, Mischief, began as an improv troupe while we were still training at LAMDA. Thirteen of the twenty-nine of us who sat on the scuffed, beige dance matting took an improvised show up to the Edinburgh Fringe the very next summer. We were green and the show was rough and ready to say the least. I remember one slightly unfortunate promo performance for a small family audience where an upbeat, ukulele song about a monkey on a bus took an unintended dark turn...

'Monkey on a bus!
Monkey on a bus!

Don't know what the fuss is,
Don't know what the fuss is,
Now the policeman's ended all the monkey's fun
    with a gun,
The monkey's dead.'

The family whose four-year-old daughter had suggested 'Monkey on a Bus' as a song title immediately walked out. We managed to keep the other four or five families in the room until Bert the Bus Conductor was asked what he kept in his special magic box, to which (under the pressure of performance) he responded, 'Dead women.' The remaining families exited and the gig finished there.

At LAMDA, Adam talked much about learning through failure, and we certainly did that day. But that Edinburgh show of ours was the beginning of a journey that was to change my life completely. Over the following years, Mischief began to grow, members came and went, some stayed on at LAMDA, and some went on to train elsewhere, but we always got together every weekend to work on our improv craft. We began doing shows in London and headed back to Edinburgh every summer.

Mischief now does less performance improv and more scripted comedy, but improv in many ways sits at the heart of everything we do. It was our formative years doing improv that allowed us to discover the comedy dynamics that worked best for us and to develop a group chemistry. All our new scripts are workshopped before going into production and through improv a huge amount of new material is discovered. Thanks to our improv work we learned the principles of storytelling that we use in our writing to this day.

In 2017, we presented *Mischief Movie Night* in the West End, a reworking of our early film-themed improv show *Lights! Camera! Improvise!* We asked Adam to come on board as improvisation consultant; we'd worked with him on other projects since LAMDA but it was wonderful to look at improv with him again. He had a wealth of new exercises and a slightly different but finely honed approach to the subject, which he fully explores in this book. An approach that focuses less on the 'dos and don'ts' and more on developing practical skills in areas of performance that improvisers need. Looking at status, storytelling and scene work, letting the improv take care of itself. It's a practical guide that strips away the cult-like mystique that improv is often shrouded in and provides an accessible handbook that anyone can learn from.

Adam has taken improv further forward than anyone else in the UK. In the book Adam quotes his mentor Ken Campbell as saying, 'There's no point improvising unless it's better than scripted stuff!' Adam's winning of the 2016 Olivier Award in a category consisting otherwise entirely of scripted work is surely a lasting testament to the fact that he and the Showstoppers have achieved this.

Mischief Theatre was founded in 2008 by a group of graduates from the London Academy of Music & Dramatic Art. The company's scripted and improvised comedy has been performed in the West End, across the UK, on Broadway and on all continents barring Antarctica! Notable productions include The Play That Goes Wrong (*Best New Comedy, Olivier Awards 2015*), The Comedy About A Bank Robbery *and* Peter Pan Goes Wrong. *From Autumn 2019 the company had a residency in the West End at the Vaudeville Theatre featuring* Groan Ups *and* Magic Goes Wrong, *created with Penn & Teller. Their first full-length TV series,* The Goes Wrong Show, *was broadcast from Christmas 2019. Mischief Theatre is led by Artistic Director Henry Lewis and Company Director Jonathan Sayer.*

Preface

This book will help you to improvise narrative drama and comedy in a group on stage. If you are new to this subject, it will guide you through the principles and techniques from scratch. For those with more experience it provides an opportunity to re-examine how improvisation is studied and practised, addressing a number of misunderstandings and confusions, while broadening the approach to, and awareness of, the subject in general. It is also aimed at groups working with or without guidance, and teachers for classes of all ages and levels of experience.

Feel free to skip ahead past the games/exercises and come back to them when relevant.

A note

Some people call it *impro*, some call it *improv*.

I have opted for *improv*, for no other reason than I prefer the sound of the word.

Acknowledgements

Thanks to all my fellow Showstoppers, who have been both school and dojo for over a decade, especially Ruth Bratt, Pippa Evans, Lucy Trodd, Philip Pellew, Andrew Pugsley, Justin Brett, Lauren Shearing, Ali James, Susan Harrison, Heather Urqhart, Julie Clare, Joshua Jackson, Jonathan Ainscough, Matt Cavendish, Duncan Walsh Atkins, Christopher Ash, Jordan Clarke, Pete Furniss, Yshani Perinpanayagam, Alex Atty, Craig Apps, Damian Roberston, Keith Strachan, Ray Cooney, Suzanna Rosenthal, Julius Green, and many others.

To The School of Night, The Society of Strange, Die-Nasty, Rapid Fire Theatre, Det Andre Teatret, I Bugiardini, Austentatious, and the astounding players of the annual London Improvathons. Also to Steve Roe of Hoopla and Andy Yeoh at BIT.

To the extraordinary Mischief Theatre, whose roots go back to LAMDA where I started studying and teaching this subject, and to those at LAMDA who encouraged the development and exploration of improv in the classroom – Joanna Read, Rodney Cottier, Anthony Ingle and Caroline Leslie.

To dear friends from overseas (again too many to mention) – Belinda Cornish, Mark Meer, Patti Stiles, Jeff Haslam, Dana Andersen, Davina Stewart, Stephanie Wolfe, Colin Mochrie, Kory Matthewson, Jamie Cavanagh, Jacob Banigan, Kayla Lorette, Amy Shostak, Kurt Smeaton, Donovan Workun and Mike McShane.

For their help, advice, and some inspirational contributions – Alan Cox, Dylan Emery, Sean McCann, Becky Johnson, Matt Schuurman, Fabrizio Lobello, Terry Johnson and Kirsten Foster.

To Matt Applewhite at Nick Hern Books for his expertise (and patience!).

To Ken Campbell – the great seeker and spur.

And my special thanks to Paul Cronin for his rigour, insight and support.

1.
Improvising

A confession: I used to hate improvisation.

I was sixteen. I just didn't get it. It seemed to be an arena where people competed to be the funniest or the loudest and, being neither, I assumed it wasn't for me.

I enjoyed watching the popular TV show *Whose Line Is It Anyway?*, but other improvisation I saw was scrappy at best and smug at worst, so I opted to continue my journey along the well-trodden path of 'proper' theatre instead.

In 2004 I met legendary British theatre maverick Ken Campbell, who had recently returned from the Canadian city of Edmonton, Alberta, where he saw a troupe called Die-Nasty perform an improvised soap opera. 'It was better than scripted stuff,' declared Ken, and it rekindled his interest in making-things-up-on-the-spot. Ken fondly remembered Keith Johnstone and the Theatre Machine in the 1960s, when improvised performance could be seen regularly at the Royal Court Theatre in London.

Ken had been commissioned by Mark Rylance to create an entertainment for the 2005 Shakespeare birthday celebrations at Shakespeare's Globe. He'd been revisiting improv with actors in Liverpool and now, gathering a small group of performers in London, Ken challenged us to improvise in the style of Shakespeare. Emulating the Bard was not enough – the aim was to improve upon the original.

This enterprise wasn't as unusual as you might think. Elizabethan acting troupes often extemporised around well-known stories, continuing a tradition passed down from the travelling players of the Italian *Commedia dell'Arte*. Hamlet warns his players: 'Let those that play your clowns speak no more than is set down for them' (Act Three, Scene Two). Evidently, improv was common back then, especially when clowning around.

For actor, director and stage designer Edward Gordon Craig, improvising lay at the very heart of the debate about Shakespearean authorship: 'I believe that the improvisators – and the comedians of that day were great improvisators – contributed a great deal to the Comedies, and not a little to several of the Tragedies. I believe the plays *grew* to their present literary perfection.'[1] For Craig, what he called 'part authorship of the world's masterpieces'[2] could be attributed directly to actors.

Perhaps improvising Shakespeare wasn't only *possible*, but was, in fact, *normal*.

The four initial workshops with Ken in a North London squat were so enlightening and enjoyable that I organised regular gatherings so our group could continue the work. The celebration at Shakespeare's Globe was called *Shall We Shog?* and featured teams from London, Liverpool and Newcastle in bouts of 'competitive poltroonery.' Mark Rylance got hit by an apple thrown from the yard. I leapt about with dancing dogs. It was a riot – wild, edgy and entertaining. Everything theatre is supposed to be.

1. Edward Gordon Graig, *The Theatre – Advancing*, Little, Brown and Company, 1919, p. 115
2. *Ibid.*

I carried on improvising and my life changed direction completely. I had quite forgotten about 'proper' theatre.

The Canadian Die-Nasty players hold an annual fifty-hour *Soap-a-Thon*. Yes, a completely improvised show lasting fifty hours, starting on a Friday evening and finishing on Sunday night. Some of the performers, musicians and technicians stay awake for the entire event, playing right the way through two consecutive nights, in order to access what they refer to as the 'lizard brain'. The sleep deprivation makes participants too tired to censor themselves or worry about anything any more, resulting in a euphoric and liberated playing style. In 2005 Ken and his manager Colin Watkeys arranged for Die-Nasty veterans Dana Andersen and Davina Stewart to fly over from Edmonton and direct a (mere) thirty-six-hour tryout with about twenty performers, hosted by the Inn On The Green in Ladbroke Grove, London. Dana had worked with inspirational American improv pioneer Del Close for many years but our experience of improvising was minimal. How were we to create a day-and-a-half of drama off the cuff?

Well, the vital thing was to say 'yes' to each other, to stop arguing and build our scenes by working in agreement. This was challenging because our instincts led us to conflict and argument, which we felt would make for interesting drama. It didn't. During one of the short breaks, Dana implored us:

- *Don't ever say 'no'.*
- *Work around it.*
- *Do not say the word 'no'.*
- *Leave it out of your vocabulary.*
- *Saying 'yes' will bring surprises and will dig you deeper.*
- *Saying 'yes' will make the world open up.*

I also observed how Dana – who directed by calling set-ups for each scene – frequently recalled events and motifs that had happened earlier (which I later learned was *reincorporation* or a *callback*) and how there was no such thing as a mistake. 'A mistake is a gift from the improv gods,' declared Dana. We couldn't make a mistake. We were free. I had never experienced anything like it.

In those thirty-six hours I was exposed to (I won't say *learned* exactly) the basics of improvisation.

For the first time I realised improvising was a craft that anyone could learn, and wondered why it hadn't been more widely taught in schools, drama schools, colleges and universities. I wondered why I hadn't done more of it, and why my reference and understanding was limited to *Whose Line Is It Anyway?* I wondered why it had almost no commercial profile in Britain, despite the thriving scenes in Canada and the US, which were feeding straight into mainstream comedy, film and television.

The following year we performed a series of shows with Ken at the Royal Court Theatre for its fiftieth-anniversary celebrations: *Décor Without Production,* performed on the sets of whatever plays were running at the time. Ken sat downstage-right with a little table, usually surrounded by books and esoteric knick-knacks, and set a series of improvised challenges to a cast of six or seven players – games (a scene where nobody can use the letter 'E'); songs (in the style of Stephen Sondheim); and short plays (inspired by whatever Ken was reading at the time – back then ventriloquism and Tuvan throat-singing were particular preoccupations of his).

I was often paired with a member of the audience or a guest who knew nothing about being on stage. Part of my task was 'to make them look good' (another popular improv maxim, as I would later learn), to support them, give them confidence and somehow steer them into making impressive tableaux.

Still lacking any real craft in improv, my preparation technique for these shows was to get drunk.

'There's no point improvising unless it's better than scripted stuff!' challenged Ken. He wasn't suggesting the resultant content, if transcribed, should be better than something a writer had time to refine and polish (although that seems no bad thing to aspire to). Instead, Ken was referring to the *spirit* of the enterprise. Audiences, knowing the performers were making everything up in the moment, could refresh their appreciation of theatre's essential quality – its *liveness*.

It was also a mantra to encourage excellence. The nervous novice improvises while signalling: 'Don't judge me, because I'm making this up as I go along.' But to make improvised performance really count, the performer has to be *more* committed, *more* dedicated, *braver*.

The clarion call for bravery spoke to me most at this time.

Over the following decade, improvisation enjoyed a surge in popularity in the UK. I am thrilled to be a part of this revival, as co-creator and director of *Showstopper! The Improvised Musical*, which started out in a tiny Portakabin at the 2008 Edinburgh Festival Fringe and went on to run in London's West End. I am also the consultant director on *Austentatious: An Improvised Jane Austen Novel* and *Mischief Movie Night*, both of which played West End runs in 2018 (*Mischief Movie Night* was nominated in the Best New Comedy category at the Olivier Awards). Improvisation was becoming prominent in mainstream theatre again. Dozens of new groups were being formed, teachers from North America were visiting the UK more regularly, and training centres for the study and practice of improv started to emerge. When *Showstopper!* first went to Edinburgh there were about a dozen improvised shows on the Fringe. Within ten years that number had risen to over one hundred, and requests were made for improvisation to have its own section in the Fringe programme. A UK improv scene was burgeoning. However, so too was confusion over its study and practice.

When I started improvising I performed instinctively, with little craft, but with plenty of guts and bravado. Later I realised I had lost the naive, joyous fearlessness of the novice who doesn't yet know how much there is to know.

I read voraciously, only to discover that many books about improv recycle the same ideas that have been around for the past forty years. Most alarmingly, the developing language and methodology is increasingly detached from acting and theatre, as if performing without a script isn't really acting at all, and presenting oneself on stage doesn't need to relate to any understanding of theatre. When improvisation ignores its heritage – dramatic construction, stagecraft, acting technique – it becomes a self-regarding indulgence more for the benefit of its players than its audiences.

I also felt the subject was frequently being mistaught. Instruction was, and to a large degree still is, based on what has gone before rather than what might be possible. I encountered a number of teachers and students alike hampered by an unhealthy obsession with rules.

I have learned to be suspicious of anyone who advocates a 'right way' or even a 'best way' to improvise. In fact, the more dogmatic the approach, the more suspicious I become, although I can understand why such approaches prove popular. In a subject so broad and filled with unknowns, the aggressive didact appears to provide *certainty*, much like religious leaders or life coaches who sidestep important and difficult debates by providing 'the definitive answer'. Guruism, usually self-declared, is on the rise in improvisation.

While writing and researching this book I became acutely aware of how much disagreement there is over terminology. Some of the language we use to define and discuss improvisation is outdated and requires revision. Like any art, improvisation is constantly evolving. As Viola Spolin, one of the progenitors of the subject in its modern form, observes: 'Styles of theater change radically with the passing of years, for the techniques of the theater are the techniques of communicating.'[3] This perpetual state of flux can be unsettling, hence not only is there differentiation of terminology but increased fervour amid practitioners to *own* elements of the practice or *have the right answer*. Some instructors are so audacious as to declare that their way is the *true* way, and I have heard many projects dismissed because they are not considered to be *pure* improvisation, as if advocating a eugenics programme for playfulness.

As Dana Andersen once said to me with a weary sigh: 'Ahhh, you know, sometimes you meet these folk who think they invented pretending.'

It's all pretending. Nobody *owns* pretending and only a fool or a charlatan would claim their way was the only way. There are countless ways to paint pictures and make music.

This book is a re-examination of the whole subject.

You might know nothing about improvisation and be exploring it without preconceptions. You might be influenced by Del Close, the founder of Chicago's Second City, who inspired generations of comedians, writers and movie stars in America, or Keith Johnstone, whose journey took him from being a London art teacher to the foundation of Loose Moose in Calgary. You might be excited by Tina Fey, Amy Poehler and the Upright Citizens Brigade of New York City, or intrigued by the early experimental theatre techniques of Viola Spolin. Maybe you studied clowning at Lecoq in Paris or with Philippe Gaulier, or did improv with a drama group, at college, or on a course. Or you enjoy quickfire comedy like *Whose Line?*, or the archetype mask-plays of the *Commedia dell'Arte*...

---

3. Viola Spolin, *Improvisation for the Theater*, Third Edition, Northwestern University Press, p. 14.

…or some other theatrical practice I've never heard of.

No one way is better than any other. It's about what you enjoy and, ultimately, what you are trying to achieve.

Improvisation is ancient. We have been 'making things up on the spot' for much longer than we have been writing things down. You improvise most of your daily life. You don't go around with a script and sometimes you don't even have a plan. Improvisation is natural and most people do it easily without realising it. But when placed in front of others and asked to entertain, without script or preparation, many will experience anxiety, tension and stress. What if, amid all those seemingly infinite possibilities, you do something *wrong*? Or boring? Or what if you reveal something about yourself? Is that bad?

This book is designed to make things simpler. With so many methods, approaches, schools of thought and techniques out there, I'm going to focus on the few basic principles that work for *all* forms of improvised performance. And I'm also providing a guide for those of you planning to work in *narrative improvisation* – in other words, how groups of performers can spontaneously create stories, plays and other theatrical presentations that stand alongside their scripted counterparts.

Nobody learns improv overnight. And it may not be a skill that one can ever master. Jeff Haslam of Die-Nasty once said to me: 'It's not possible to be an expert in this subject.' I agree.

A book can only be a guide. You have to get onto a stage and try things out with other people. The American writer/ director David Mamet reminds us that reading everything there is to read about the history of boxing won't help us in the ring.

Your journey, of course, is your own. I can't say which methods and techniques will work best for you, but I can share my experiences and what I have learned along the way. My focus at all times will be on the most basic principles, without which all improvisers are lost.

In the introduction to his book *The Crafty Art of Playmaking*, Alan Ayckbourn issues a 'mild apology'[4] that most of the examples he gives throughout are drawn from his own plays. While I share his fears of self-aggrandisement, I can assure you that I also share his motives; life lessons are often more usefully drawn from personal experience (and are easier to remember). As such, I refer to shows I have been most closely involved in as a player and/or director, namely: *Showstopper! The Improvised Musical*, the *London Fifty-Hour Improvathons*, *The School of Night* and *Rhapsodes,* my work with Canadian companies Die-Nasty and Rapid Fire Theatre, as well as the UK's own *Mischief Movie Night* and *Austentatious*. I will also refer to other shows and practitioners along the way. You don't need to have seen any of these productions to understand the points being illustrated.

Much of the work in this book was developed at the London Academy of Music and Dramatic Art (LAMDA), where I have been teaching since 2004. Some of the exercises are my own and were developed in the classroom, some have been developed from the work of other practitioners and teachers, and some come from long-established sources which remain relevant and effective.

Improvising can be hugely enjoyable. It often creates an environment where groups of people can share ideas, find consensus with each other and support risk-taking, while encouraging growth and expression for the individual and the community. There is much to discover and enjoy for the professional performer and hobbyist alike. Some become evangelical about it (British improv pioneer Jim Sweeney refers to such enthusiasts as 'born-again improvisers'). Many

4. Alan Ayckbourn, *The Crafty Art of Playmaking*, Faber and Faber, 2002, p. viii.

proudly declare 'improv changed my life'. There are teachers who boldly promise that 'learning improv will make you a better person'.

I won't make you that promise (who can? I mean, really?). But I do know that fun without discipline can be indulgence, and the more disciplined my work is, the more I enjoy it.

Whether you are looking to get involved in all this for the first time, or if you already have some experience but want to deepen your understanding of this exciting, stimulating and ever-evolving art form – read on.

Terminology

Improvisation essentially means 'unrehearsed', 'spontaneous', 'created in the moment'. In other words – 'making it up as you go along'.

Before investigating the work of Spolin, Johnstone, Close et al., I had only ever encountered improvisation as an actor in the rehearsal room. A director might say: 'Okay, put the scripts down and just improvise the scene in your own words,' or we would be developing a new play with the writer present and asked to explore different scenarios by improvising them. We would try things out, have a discussion, and then try again with new instructions. Most actors or students of theatre will be familiar with these ways of working.

I call this *development improvisation*. Here, improv is used to refine, rework and improve a final scripted product. The elements of improvisation remain private to the rehearsal room or studio, and are not seen by a paying audience. (The filmmaker Mike Leigh famously commits to many months of improvisation with his actors in order to generate a finished screenplay.)

In *performance improvisation*, the performers engage the audience without a script and often with nothing prepared or rehearsed in advance. Dialogue, plot, action and characters can all be either entirely improvised or improvised around a few predetermined ideas. For example, in *Austentatious* the performers know they will play in the style of Jane Austen; their set and costumes are all prepared, but they have no idea what the story, characters or dialogue will be. Inspiration for the content of these shows tends to come from the audience, which is often asked for suggestions by the performers: 'Where does this scene take place?' or 'What is this story called?'

This book is about *performance improvisation*, although an understanding of its basic principles and techniques will help immeasurably with *development improvisation*.

◊ ◊ ◊

Broadly speaking, there are three types of *performance improvisation – shortform, longform* and *narrative*.[5] These are all terms currently being used by improvisers (in the UK, at least).

In researching this book I asked twenty improvisers, from different countries, backgrounds and levels of experience, to define the three terms above.

No two answers were the same.

So, in the interests of simplification and clarity, permit me to suggest some basic definitions.

---

5. I'm not including immersive theatre here, although it undoubtedly involves elements of improvisation.

Shortform

- Games and scenes that don't have any narrative connection with each other.

- The emphasis tends towards comedic entertainment, although these scenes and games can explore any kind of theme or content.

- Audiences are usually asked to provide some information immediately before every scene or game, e.g. 'What genre is this scene in?' or 'What is the relationship between these two characters?'

Whose Line Is It Anyway? and Keith Johnstone's *Theatresports*™ are well-known examples of shortform.

Longform

- Scenes connect into an overall story or stories.
- In most longforms, performers ask the audience for a single word at the start of the presentation in order to inspire everything that follows.

The most famous longform is called the Harold, although there are many others, including the Armando and La Ronde.

The *form* in shortform could be a game, a scene, or a song.

Whatever form it takes, it's *short* – unlikely to last more than a few minutes.

The *form* in longform refers to structures and scene patterns that all players must agree on in advance in order to perform it. And it will be longer than a few minutes, with most commercial presentations typically lasting between thirty and seventy minutes.

The Harold, created by Del Close and Charna Halpern (and subsequently developed by many others), was initiated as a way of incorporating shortform games and scenes into an overall story. A traditional Harold is structured as follows:

1. A group shortform game is followed by three scenes (1A, 1B, 1C).

2. Then another shortform game is played, followed by the furtherance of the three original scenes (2A, 2B, 2C).

3. A third game is followed by the conclusion of those recurring scenes (3A, 3B, 3C).

Numerous variants of the Harold have developed over time, but that's the basic structure all players must be familiar with. Other longforms have structures too, some more complex, some less so.

Confused? Don't worry. This is not a book about how to do a Harold. But the ideas and exercises herein apply to any kind of longform improvisation.

Narrative

In *longform*, the players explore a story using a predetermined structure.

In *narrative*, the players explore a story without any predetermined structure.

One could argue that all improvisation is narrative. Even a short scene tells some kind of story: connect any events and story begins to emerge. I have also heard the phrases 'open longform' and 'free longform' used to denote longform presentations without set structures, but the term *narrative improvisation* is increasingly being used in the UK and Europe. If you are presenting a play, musical or story without predetermined plan or structure, I'm suggesting the term *narrative improvisation*.

Showstopper! The Improvised Musical doesn't follow a predetermined structure. The company, in fact, is *discovering* what kind of story it is telling as the performance unfolds. *Mischief Movie Night* establishes what genre of movie it will emulate (thriller, romantic comedy, documentary, etc.), and the players forge a story inspired by the requirements of that genre.

Improv can be comic, tragic, tragicomic, theatrical, meta-theatrical, genre-based, naturalistic, heightened, farcical, satirical, clown, absurdist, for the camera, for the stage, or a mixture of any of these elements (and more), but it still fundamentally operates within the principles of drama and storytelling.

Now here's the rub…

Many groups are, to their detriment, using *shortform* techniques to create *longform* and *narrative* improvisation.

Both brush and chisel can be used to create art, but one is better suited to the canvas and the other better suited to sculpture. It's time to re-examine improvisation and figure out which tools work best for which purposes, to discover which tools are mislabelled or no longer useful, and to understand the guiding principles that, ultimately, all techniques serve.

2.
The Moment

Many actors regard 'being in the moment' as the Holy Grail of acting. You might be familiar with the phrase: 'Don't act – just be.' Improvised performance also reveres this desire to be present and react spontaneously. But if you are about to do a workshop with someone who claims they can teach you how to be in the moment – hold on. There are monks who have spent decades studying and meditating in the pursuit of being in the moment, and many of them will tell you that they are just getting started. To seek to 'be in the moment' is only the beginning of a journey.

You can learn how to play poker or chess in about twenty minutes, although excellence in those games may take a further twenty years of study and practice. It is the same with acting. The basic principles and techniques employed in order to be (or appear) spontaneous are relatively simple, but years of dedicated application and experience are required.

In order to be in the moment, it helps to know what has happened prior to the moment (your 'given circumstances') and what the character wants or hopes to achieve beyond the moment (your 'intention'). The immediate past and imminent future are like bookends, structures that support and inform the actor in the present. Of the infinite possibilities as to how one might behave, reactions in the moment are primarily informed by what you *want* and what you *know*. Macbeth is startled when informed that the King is about to make him Thane of Cawdor because he *knows* the witches told him this would happen. Lady Macbeth inspires her husband to commit regicide because she *wants* him to become King. What we know of the past and what we want in the future help us understand how to be in the moment. All well and good when the lines are written down and the scene is rehearsed and analysed, but when the improviser doesn't have any lines and doesn't know what's going to happen next, what then?

Actor/director Konstantin Stanislavsky, in recalling his early years upon the stage, remembers how many factors were contributing to his self-consciousness. His lines, his gestures, the costumes and lighting, his awareness of being watched by an audience, his own thought processes as he was performing, plus numerous other elements you have no doubt experienced if you have been on stage or screen. His eventual discovery, one of the vital tenets of acting, was that it helps to know where to put your attention.

Outward focus is the key to all effective acting, be it with or without a script.

Rules v. Principles

'A thousand techniques are inferior to the single principle.'

David Mamet, quoting a ju-jitsu master

I used to teach a course at a film school helping directors to work with actors. Many of the participants could communicate easily with their technical departments (camera, sound, etc.) but when it came to interacting with actors they lacked the skills or vocabulary to be effective.

My approach was to take an overview of the subject of acting, examining various processes used by actors, exploring some helpful terminology and basic principles that apply to any situation.

The analogy might be: 'We need to learn about *agriculture*. What is soil and how should it be treated? What is its chemical composition? How is it affected by weather and climate? How do seeds grow? What is required to cultivate them?'

The course participants were impatient. They wanted quick answers and easy fixes, and didn't want to engage with the principles behind the subject. They weren't interested in understanding the bigger picture about agriculture, they wanted me to teach them how to use the shiny new tractor they had seen someone using recently.

My response was to say: 'I can give you the shiny new tractor but what will you do if it breaks down? Do you know how the machinery relates to soil, chemical balance and climate? Will you know when to upgrade your tractor and what to replace it with?'

There are numerous techniques in improvisation, and knowing them helps you build a diverse toolkit as a performer. But if you don't know the principles behind the work then you won't know how or when to use those tools.

Many of the so-called 'rules of improvisation' can create tension and confusion for the student. Separated from the *principles* of improvisation, rules become burdens, usually experienced by the novice as something they must remember under pressure.

Those of you who have studied improvisation may have encountered a number of these rules:

- *Don't ask questions.*
- *Don't block.*

- *Don't change your point of view.*

- *Don't think.*

It's strange for a subject that is essentially about freedom of choice and expression to have so many rules beginning with the word *don't*.

Screenwriting instructor Robert McKee reminds us that 'Anxious, inexperienced writers obey rules. Rebellious, unschooled writers break rules. Artists master the form.'[6]

Rules are created during exploration. They are a reaction to investigation and discovery, used variously to protect, guide and nurture better practice and understanding. They are forged under very particular circumstances and are inevitably better suited to some situations than others.

The rule 'don't ask questions' developed in response to a fear of decision-making in scenes. The novice improviser, observing their fellow performer miming some sort of activity, politely enquires as to what they are doing. Uncertain of their situation, they put pressure on other players to provide clarity. This kind of politeness and caution can kill a scene. Once the improviser is instead encouraged to make a statement – 'That's a great fire you're building', 'You're getting good at origami' – the scene proceeds with confidence. Confidence is important. It helps the audience feel secure. Audiences don't want to feel fearful for a performer. Seeing the performer *in trouble and danger* can be entertaining but a visibly nervous performer lacking in confidence is unsettling.

Of course you can have scenes with questions. Drama is filled with questions and debate. You can have scenes comprised entirely of questions if you wish. Try it out. Play a scene where the participants *only* ask questions and are not allowed to make statements. This can also be played as a competitive

---

6. Robert McKee, *Story: Substance, Structure, Style, and the Principles of Screenwriting*, Methuen, 1999, p. 3.

game. Two players, without hesitation, repetition or non sequitur, must play a scene comprised only of questions. As soon as someone fails to ask a question, or stalls, they are eliminated and a new player takes their place.

Instead of fixating on the rule we should consider the principles behind it. Try replacing: 'Don't ask questions' with 'A statement can be more effective than a question.'

As you continue your investigation into improvisation, take anything that has been offered as a rule and put it to the test. Try playing scenes adhering to the rule and try playing scenes where you intentionally break it. Seek, as McKee says, to understand the *form*.

Anything offered as a rule should undergo rigorous testing.

Three Basic Principles
Listening
Accepting
Committing

1. Listening

Listening, attention and behaviour

The best definition of listening I know comes from improvisers:

> 'Listening is the willingness to be changed.'

Listening, for our purposes, is not solely aural. It is not merely retaining words or information. Listening requires paying attention to the demeanour and behaviour of others like a poker player looking for tells. Effective observation sparks impulses in the observer. These impulses are the lifeblood of your work.

All forms of drama, scripted or otherwise, require characters to affect each other. Real listening is the willingness to be affected and changed by what is said or done.

Improv is often analysed in terms of what people say, rather than what people are doing and how they are doing it. But observation of behaviour is essential because the majority of our communication is non-verbal.

A *and* B *are holding hands.*

A. I'm crazy about you.

B *(withdrawing her hand and presenting him with a terse smile).* That's wonderful.

B's *behaviour* here tells us more than the words do.

The American acting teacher Sanford Meisner, who developed a methodology for training actors based on observation and repetition, said: 'Acting is not talking. It is living off the other fellow.'[7]

Outward focus is the key to all effective acting.

---

7. Sanford Meisner and Dennis Longwell, *Sanford Meisner on Acting*, Vintage, 1987, p. 42.

The audience is fully aware of (in fact, finely tuned to) a performer's behaviour. The improviser, however, loses this self-awareness when worrying about what to do next or when uncertain about where to focus their attention.

Listening exercises and games

Many of the exercises created by Sanford Meisner are documented in his book *Sanford Meisner on Acting*. Here's one from my time spent in class with Meisner Technique teacher Scott Williams.

The 'Three Moment' Game

Two players (A and B) sit opposite each other, comfortable and relaxed, a few feet apart.

A observes B and makes a simple, obvious, factual observation about B.

- You have black hair.
- You are wearing glasses.
- You have a white shirt.
- Your hair is tied back.

A's observation is *moment one*.

For this exercise, players should avoid speculative or emotional offers such as:

- I think you are angry.
- You look like you are thinking about something sad.
- You clearly don't like this game.

Stick to simple, factual observations – the more obvious, the better. And it's fine to say something you have already said earlier. Each moment is fresh, disassociated from the last, so say what you see in it.

B then repeats what A has said from their point of view (i.e. in the first person). They are not trying to interpret the line or do any 'performing'. This is *moment two* – a simple repetition:

A (*moment one*). You are wearing glasses.

B (*moment two*). I am wearing glasses.

In *moment three*, A says what they observed B doing in moment two.

A (*moment one*). You are wearing glasses.

B (*moment two*). I am wearing glasses.

A (*moment three*). You shifted in your chair and touched your glasses with your hand.

Keep it simple and mechanical. Say the most obvious thing. This exercise is not about encouraging imagination or creativity, it's about putting one's attention on the other person.

After moment three we start afresh but switch, so that B now speaks first, making an observation of A. A then repeats what B just said (moment two), and B then describes what they saw A doing in moment two.

A game may run something like this:

A. Your hair is tied back.

B. My hair is tied back.

A. You smiled.

...

B. You are wearing a black T-shirt.

A. I'm wearing a black T-shirt.

B. You nodded your head and lifted your right foot.

...

A. Your hands are folded in your lap.

B. My hands are folded in my lap.

A. You moved your hands.

...

B. You have an earring.

A. I have an earring.

B. You smiled and sat back in your chair.

Continue to play for a few minutes. This exercise requires repeated practice.

When playing for the first time with a new group I might need to call out each moment as it occurs: 'One, two, three. Switch and start again. One, two, three,' etc.

Things to look out for

Be aware of unnecessary tension. You don't have to scrutinise your partner with a scowl, searching for something original to comment on. Simply say the most obvious thing you see, even if you have said it before.

Players, in moment three, might comment that their partner didn't really do anything in moment two. However, there is always something going on.

For example:

- You looked at me.
- You spoke.
- You repeated what I said.
- You held your body very still.

You may find players become tired very quickly. They are not always used to this level of listening or being so intimately connected with another person.

Try to keep the observations in the world of the positive rather than the negative: 'You were very still' rather than 'You didn't move.' Say what *is* there, not what *isn't*.

Instincts to subvert the game or force things to happen will emerge. Keep the exercise as simple and uninflected as possible.

With practice the game becomes lighter, quicker and easier.

One tenet of David Mamet's *True and False* (one of the best books on acting I know) is 'Invent nothing. Deny nothing.'[8]

By being outwardly focused and voicing their observations, the improviser doesn't have to worry about what they are creating ('invent nothing') and is freely responding to their impulses ('deny nothing'). Listening is the first step towards achieving this.

Improvisation isn't about what you create and generate so much as what you allow to happen.

2. Accepting

On Agreement

> 'Can this cockpit hold
> The vasty fields of France? Or may we cram
> Within this wooden O, the very casques
> That did affright the air at Agincourt?'

> Chorus, Prologue, *Henry V*

How do we take a blank stage with no set or scenery and turn it into 'the vasty fields of France'? Or a New York diner? Or a cruise ship, an office block, a swanky hotel, eighteenth-century Versailles, the Liverpool docks?

Those famous opening lines from *Henry V* go straight to the heart of how theatre works. They are an invitation for an audience to play a game with the performers, a game where we *agree*. The performers put forward a proposal – 'What if we were actually in France?' – and the audience is invited to agree, to pretend along with the actors. We create a consensus for reality. Note the words *'what if?'* as a vital tool for imaginative engagement in theatre and acting.

---

8. David Mamet, *True and False: Heresy and Common Sense for the Actor*, Faber and Faber, 1998, p. 24.

In improvisation, the performers agree with each other's suggestions to create every aspect of the reality of the scene – setting, character, relationship, mood, genre, tempo, etc. The characters can be in conflict, or even in differing realities (which we'll come to later), but the actors must work in agreement with each other. This agreement to play lies at the core of all theatrical forms.

Defy this principle and you make it very difficult for the audience to engage with you.

On 'Yes' and 'No'

If you have done any kind of improvisation, you will have come across the phrase 'Yes, and…'. For some it's a mantra, for others it's an unbreakable rule. 'Yes' embodies the spirit of improv and 'no' is considered a 'block'.

Such approaches are oversimplistic and inevitably problematic.

'Yes' relates to building something with your fellow players, a desire to create and develop collaboratively. 'And' relates to the *forward movement of the scene*.

'Yes, and…' facilitates *collective progression*.

Note that 'Yes, and…' was designed for shortform improv over sixty years ago and it remains an effective tool for that format. A novice player can accept ideas and build upon them, thereby making progress quickly:

    A. Nice day for tennis.

    B. *Yes, and* this time I brought the rackets we had when we were kids.

    A. Did you just get fired?

    B. *Yes, and* they want you to take over my job.

    A. Your sister told me you're starting a band.

    B. *Yes, and* I need a drummer. Interested?

But be warned: 'Yes, and...' isn't the whole story, and misunderstanding its application frequently causes trouble in longform and narrative improvisation.

There is a difference between *saying* 'yes' and engaging with the essence of the offer. I have seen many players say 'yes' dutifully because they are trying to be good improvisers. This kind of mechanical 'yes' is difficult to deal with because the player is disconnected from the moment and unaffected by the offer. When a player gives a mechanical 'yes', they are psychologically stuck in the classroom, not present in the moment of performance.

'Yes, and...' is a principle for improvisers to work with, not necessarily words the characters in a scene should say.

A real 'yes' is *to be affected by the offer*, whether you actually use the word 'yes' or not. Remember – listening is the willingness to be changed.

    A. Do you want to make yourself comfortable?

    B. Yes. (*Doesn't move or change position.*)

Actor B has listened to actor A and verbally agreed with them, but has not been changed or affected by the offer.

    A. Do you want to make yourself comfortable?

    B. I'm afraid I can't stay long. (*Sighs, smiles, stretches out, and kicks off shoes.*)

Here actor B not only accepts A's offer and is affected by it immediately, but also delivers a line of dialogue contrasting with their physical activity. B claims not to be able to stay for long, but B's behaviour – the stretching out and kicking off of shoes – implies the opposite. This contradiction also reveals something of B's character.

Shortform comedy is helped by making connections quickly and the discovery of *games* within the scene.

But any kind of sustained narrative will require *dramatic tension*. The use of 'yes' or 'no' only matters in how it serves that tension. There are many narratives that would be ruined by 'Yes, and...'

Imagine the following from Shakespeare's *Macbeth*:

> MACBETH. We will proceed no further in this business.
>
> LADY M. *Yes, and* we should accept our social status in Scotland.

Or from Chekhov's *Three Sisters*:

> IRINA. Let's go to Moscow.
>
> SISTERS. *Yes, and* our bags are already packed!

Or Beckett's *Waiting for Godot*:

> ESTRAGON. Will Godot ever get here?
>
> VLADIMIR. *Yes, and* here he is now.

Besides, in many stories the protagonist initially resists their 'call to adventure' (a healthy use of the word 'no'), and often learns to give up what they thought they wanted most. The improviser who has been trained to say 'yes' no matter what the situation may miss or negate opportunities for interesting dramatic development.

There are times to say 'yes' and there are times to say 'no' and we will investigate them further throughout this book. For now, let's keep working with the concept of 'yes'.

Yes Party

The whole group mill around the entire space as if at a party. This is played as a developmental improvisation exercise, in that it doesn't require any sense of performance and players can all speak at the same time without a single clear point of focus. Players can do anything they like but they must remove the word 'no' from their vocabulary. If they say 'no' at any time, another player can say: 'Sorry, did you just say no?' – and the original player can amend accordingly: 'I'm so sorry, I meant to say yes.'

Play for five to ten minutes, then gather the group and find out what happened during the game.

With so much agreement and split focus, it tends to become quite surreal. Players agree to realities that often conflict with or even negate each other, although they usually find a way to deal with these clashes and carry on.

You will also observe that players, knowing others must now say 'yes' to their ideas, often like to put each other in trouble:

A. Oh, I know you, you're a poet, aren't you?

B. Yes, I am.

A. Can you recite a poem for me now?

B. Errr... yes, I can...

Players can qualify their responses with 'yes, and...' and 'yes, but...'

A. Oh, I know you, you're a poet, aren't you?

B. Yes, and I can see you are about to recite my most famous poem.

Or for the performer who loves to embrace trouble:

A. Oh, I know you, you're a poet, aren't you?

B. Yes, and I shall now recite my latest poem...

It's worth reminding players of these 'yes variants' in case they find themselves playing with someone who unscrupulously exploits the game's agreement that all players must say 'yes':

A. You want to kiss me, don't you?

B. Yes, *but* my husband is in the next room.

Actor B may or may not kiss actor A. It's their choice. They should not be forced to do so by the rule 'always say yes'. While we often enjoy seeing *characters* in awkward situations, accepting offers does not have to lead *players* into taking action that makes them personally uncomfortable. Compelling everyone to say 'yes' to everything all the time is the conduct of a cult, not an improv group.

Shopping Channel

Have two players stand behind a table with ten or twenty random items on it. These items can come from group members or might be found around the room you are in (water bottles, phones, wallets, keys, etc.).

The two players pretend to be presenters on a TV shopping channel and describe the items on sale, their functions and unique selling points.

A set of keys might be specialist skeleton keys that open any lock, or they might not even be keys at all. They might be the centrepiece of a brass necklace, a children's toy, or a miniature metal self-defence weapon.

A game usually lasts around three or four minutes.

Encourage the players to spend as long as possible detailing each object. Where was the object made? What's it made of? Why is it so special? What makes it this year's 'must have' accessory? How many are left in stock?

They don't have to get through all of the objects on the table; other players can have their turn with any remaining items.

This game is excellent for encouraging agreement. The shopping-channel hosts need to sell items so they never argue with each other. This game is very much driven by 'Yes, and...' (in fact, the phrase is seldom more apposite).

It's also good for practising *specifics* and *commitment* (see later).

You may wish to start with players who are familiar with the concept of a shopping channel, so that the tone and game are clear from the outset.

3. Committing

There is nowhere to hide (and no fun in hiding).

If you stand in front of an audience and declare that everything you are about to do is improvised, then you had better perform with commitment. Audiences will forgive almost everything except its lack. Why should they downgrade their expectations simply because what they are watching is improvised? A lack of commitment makes an audience insecure.

I have seen mediocre content succeed purely on the strength of the performers' delivery. I have also seen evenings of improv undone by a lack of commitment in its many forms: a lack of confidence (usually caused by a lack of basic performance skills), a lack of knowing how to communicate with an audience, or a glib playing style employed to avoid emotional engagement.

Book Launch

Have some books to hand: novels, instruction manuals, fiction, biography, history, self-help – it doesn't really matter as long as there's a mix of genres.

One player stands in front of the group and starts reading aloud from a randomly selected page of the book. After thirty seconds or so, take the book away from them. The player must continue speaking for at least another minute, as if they were still reading from the same part of the same book.

It sounds difficult but you'll be amazed at the results when players rise to the challenge.

The player should observe the mood, tone, structure of language, length of sentences, use of vocabulary and idiom, and anything else evident from the book so they can continue in the same vein. They should also recycle material, bringing back anything from the passage that was read aloud at the start (see later – *reincorporation* or *callback*).

Players often disconnect from the moment, retreat into their 'thinking space', and come up with new ideas that don't relate to what has gone before. They may even start voicing their own fears and insecurities. Encourage them to use what was initially given to them and repeat and recycle as much as possible.

There is no need to look forward in this game – only back.

Jackanapes

One player stands before the group and makes up a joke on the spot from a subject/conceit/first line given to them by the audience. They must play with complete confidence as if they actually know the joke very well.

  – Tell us the joke about the parrot and the bank
    clerk!

Hopefully the player will immediately begin as if they know the joke:

  – Okay, so this parrot goes into a bank…

Players used to writing or comedy may be able to forge a creditable joke with a punchline in the heat of the moment, and while that might be satisfying it isn't the purpose of the exercise. The game is designed to put the player in a seemingly impossible situation so that the audience can enjoy watching their commitment against the odds. So long as they keep going and make it look, sound and feel like a joke, they will maintain the audience's attention.

You may wish to wait until a group is more advanced, or more confident, before attempting this game. It can fuel one of the great anxieties of improvisation – that it must always be funny (although here the humour arises from behaviour in the face of the unknown, not from the player's ability to tell jokes or think of funny things to say).

Shopping Channel (page 33)

In order to sell those items you have to be *committed*!

Reverse Karaoke/Lip-sync

I developed this as a clown game while auditioning students for LAMDA. Select some recorded music that has one or more clear vocal parts on it, ideally something obscure that players are unlikely to have ever heard before. Performers must lip-sync to the vocal lines even though they don't know what the words are or what the tune is, or indeed anything about it at all. Nevertheless they must perform with the absolute conviction of knowing. It is, of course, impossible, but when played with commitment it's wonderfully entertaining. And the performer can experience the joy of not knowing, of commitment in the face of uncertainty, of bold performance while being in the unknown.

This game can be played with one player or small groups, depending on what music is selected. It works especially well with obscure operas and musicals.

Emotional Cinema

Ideally played with up to fifteen players.

Get the players to sit in a single row as if they are at a cinema, looking up at an imaginary screen, pretending they are watching a film. Little or no dialogue is required in this game and it is usually better without any.

On the bell,[9] players must have an immediate emotional response to something that has happened in the film. It can be any kind of response but they must *all have the same emotion*. Players will need to look at each other as the emotional reactions are changing. It's delightful to watch when the players are bold, and rather dull when they're cautious. We enjoy seeing one or two players quickly adjust their laughter to fit the rest of the crying ensemble. Being fully committed at the same time as being prepared to yield any idea at any time is critical in improvisation.

These Are Six Things

A circle game where people list things under time pressure.

The first player gives a subject, e.g. modes of transport, to the next player, who then names six things within that category before the rest of the group have counted to ten (train, bus, donkey, taxi, helicopter, sled, etc.).

Try playing *These Are Seven Things*, or as many 'things' as you dare. The group counting to ten exerts pressure on the player.

Instant Jingles

Best played with small teams of about five performers.

Give the group a fictitious product or service, such as 'Prestatyn Pet Insurance' or 'Neptune's Underwater Holidays', and have them immediately improvise the advert or jingle for it. The ad must look, sound and feel authentic. Keep them as short and snappy as adverts and jingles are. There is joy to be found in the immediacy of commitment, regardless of the outcome.

---

9. I teach classes using a desk bell like the ones you find at hotel reception. I find it provides a clear focus for when to start and when to end a scene or exercise. It's also effective for getting people to respond or act with immediacy. Some people clap their hands or use a drum – I'm fond of the bell.

Most of these commitment games are about playing under pressure, getting used to it, learning to enjoy it, or creating in spite of it.

Significance of the Three Basic Principles

I believe that a performer who has an understanding of these three principles could play in any kind of improvised performance. I have put this to the test with many year groups at LAMDA.

For ten years I ran a twenty-eight-week intensive training for students, usually aged eighteen to twenty-one, called the Foundation Course. I observed groups studying improv according to traditional rules and guidelines, and found that several bad habits developed and persisted. Students were often fretting about what they *shouldn't* do, rather than exploring what they *could* do. Although progress was made, it wasn't as swift or as effective as with the groups that had spent six to eight weeks studying Meisner Technique, or groups that worked with the principles first, subsequently discovering various techniques and disciplines as they went along. For those who had practised Meisner exercises for a few weeks before they started improvising, being able to observe and listen to each other was easy and natural, and this discipline remained evident when playing games or building scenes. Students were accepting of each other's ideas with ease and immediacy. *Focusing outwardly* and *acting on one's impulses* had already become habitual.

But What About…?

What about trust? Isn't that important? What about imagination? Surely you can't improvise without imagination? Aren't these principles too?

Well… no.

Trust can't be forced. And strangers, meeting for the first time in an improv scene, can't be expected to trust each other. You can't demand it of players. Trust is built up over time. If you want people to trust you – *listen* to them.

And everyone has an imagination. Some people are simply more aware of this than others, but everyone can imagine. Imagination is not a principle of this work – it's a function of the brain.

I've seen great scenes that were unimaginative and I have seen great scenes in which the players clearly didn't trust each other. I have also seen great scenes in which people say 'no' a lot. I have seen great scenes that break every so-called rule of improv. Maybe you have too.

The scenes I have witnessed, or been in, that are *consistently ineffective* are the ones in which performers are *playing without listening, acceptance or commitment.*

Wax On, Wax Off and Warm Up

Getting started

In *The Karate Kid*, a young man wants to learn martial arts but is frustrated when mentor Mr Miyagi makes him paint his fence and wax his car. In fact, Mr Miyagi is very specific about how he wants his car to be waxed and shows our hero the precise hand movements required: 'Wax on, wax off, wax on, wax off…' After several weeks the young man's impatience eventually gets the better of him and he snaps: 'I came here to learn martial arts, not to do your chores for you!' At which point the old teacher unleashes a flurry of attacks on the kid who instinctively parries with all the moves from his muscle memory – wax on, wax off. He has already learned without realising.

When starting with a new group, I like to get the principles into their muscle memory as early as possible. It's the improv equivalent of 'wax on, wax off'.

Ballet

I start with a ballet. I ask ten or fifteen people to perform a piece of improvised dance theatre lasting approximately five minutes while I play the piano for them. The challenge is that it must look like it has been impressively choreographed and meticulously rehearsed. In short, they must make it look like a finished product (*commit*). To do so, they can copy/mirror each other and all move in unison like a flock of birds (*listen*), or they can watch someone do a move and then copy it (*accept*), thereby creating patterns that appear to be choreographed (*pattern recognition*, see later).

I remind players that they don't all have to be on stage the whole time. Entering and exiting, giving space and focus to others, is encouraged. They can leave room for a solo or a duet. I ask for an inspiring word or concept as the title of the ballet, such as 'light', 'temptation' or 'transformation', and away we go. From the piano, I respond to their changes in energy, tempo and rhythm, and sometimes lead them with offers for new moods or emotions.

Working in the abstract physical frees players from the pressure of what to say, and this kind of group work allows them to explore the basic principles effectively.

I've done dozens of ballets with first-time groups and they have all been delightful. The aspiration makes it exciting and the commitment makes it impressive. It's an inspiring way to begin improv training. Day one, session one: a full-scale dance performance with a big group! Immediately the class gets a taste of what can be achieved through listening, agreement and commitment.

Wax on, wax off…

Nothing beats practice.

There are hundreds of starting and warm-up games, but here are a few that I find illustrate the basic principles most effectively.

Most improv games I know are best played with a light, almost childlike sense of play. Keep encouraging people not to worry. Nobody is expected to master a game they haven't played before. Like most games, they have to be played repeatedly before any competence can be developed, although in many respects competence isn't the objective. The group's shared commitment to agree and play together remains the most vital part of the experience. I try to keep the atmosphere light and humorous in these early sessions.

Soundball

Players stand in a circle. An imaginary ball of sound, voiced by the thrower (*whoosh*), is thrown across the circle towards another player. The player receives the ball with the same sound as was sent to them (*whoosh*), changes it into a different sound (*zap*), then passes it to another player, who in turn receives the same sound (*zap*), before changing it (*kadadadada*), and passing the new sound on, etc.

It should be played as fast as possible, without missing any of the beats:

- Send (with a sound).
- Receive (with the same sound).
- Change (to a new sound).
- Throw (the new sound).

The players are training in the basic principles:

1. Listening.

2. Accepting and being changed by/affected by.

3. Committing to a new offer.

Things to look out for

Keep the game light, playful and quick.

Players will bring extraordinary tensions to this game, frequently adding apologies and judgements to the process. Try to take apology and judgement out of the room for these sorts of games. Keep going until the group relaxes into the pattern:

- Send
- Receive
- Change
- Throw

After a while you can try playing with three soundballs.

Although players now experience split focus and new distractions, the process remains the same: Send – Receive – Change – Throw.

Players must make certain that someone else has accepted their offer. Was the intended receiver distracted? Does the ball need to be thrown again? Do you need to let go of your original intention and instead send the ball to someone else? This game encourages players to remain observant and connected, and see how their offers are affecting each other.

Clapping Circle

One of the best and simplest tune-in games I know.

Players stand in a fairly tight circle so that everyone can see each other clearly. The first player makes eye contact with someone else in the group and both players clap their hands at exactly the same time. Then the new player (who had been looked at by the first player) looks at someone else and they both clap their hands at the same time. And so on.

Look at someone – clap at the same time.

Keep a steady rhythm going throughout. If your target misses the clap for any reason, keep clapping on the beat, in rhythm, until they finally pick it up. In this way the game maintains a consistent pulse.

As in *Soundball*, tension and apology is rife. Encourage players to relax and observe their colleagues. There is no need for self-judgement or admonishment, although if you discuss these impulses with the group afterwards you may find that players share some interesting insights.

Players will contort their bodies with tension trying to 'get it right'. Watch out for the habitual flashes of physical tension that players make when they fear they have made any kind of error. The whole body winces and the face grimaces with the expression: 'Sorry!' As we shall observe later there is no such thing as a mistake in this work, so it is useful to address this now and begin to eliminate unnecessary, habitual tension. Keep it light.

Players begin to find their balance between over-focusing (tense, 'to get it right') and under-focusing (disengaged, uncommitted).

As you get more comfortable, see how fast you can go.

Sandwiches

I ask someone to get up into the space and be a piece of bread, saying: 'I am a piece of bread.'

Someone does so, usually standing or lying down with their arms outstretched.

Then I ask someone to join them and be a piece of cheese, saying: 'I am a piece of cheese.'

And someone does so. They might stand next to the piece of bread or lie on top of the bread, but they connect visually and physically to the other player in some way without thinking about it.

Then I ask someone else to go and be another piece of bread, saying: 'I am a piece of bread.'

And when this is done all three players, in unison, say: 'We are a cheese sandwich.'

That's the game in all its wonderful simplicity. I ask the group to play a variety of sandwiches, now initiating the game themselves without being called to the stage.

Play fast, light and without attachment to ideas or outcome.

As players start to build new sandwiches you may observe that they copy the staging that went before them and, as a result, all sandwiches are created in the same way. Encourage them to explore new ways of presenting their sandwiches on stage.

Players will begin to pack the sandwiches with so many ingredients that it's impossible to remember everything and come together at the end to speak in unison. Remind them to keep it simple.

Players often subvert the game with disgusting ingredients to try to shock or be interesting. I tend to let that slide at an early stage but note the impulse.

If two players jump up at the same time, they immediately think it is some kind of mistake and will try to sit back down. Allow the players' impulses to drive them to the stage. Any number of players can get up at the same time so long as they make their contributions one at a time.

The game is built up from single offers.

And there is no such thing as a mistake. How can there be? It's a nonsense game about sandwiches, for heaven's sake!

Players will do anything to avoid speaking in unison at the end. They will stall, delay, feel awkward, or lead too aggressively so others cannot follow. They are embarrassed if it doesn't 'work' and, once again, apology is ubiquitous.

Sandwiches and *Clapping Circle* help players follow their impulses, to play light and freely, removing tension caused by so-called errors.

Once people are playing sandwiches in a light and playful manner, open up the concept so they can build anything, one offer at a time, until they collectively agree to end by speaking in unison – in 'one voice'.

- I am a steering wheel.
- I am a roof rack.
- I am an engine.
- I am a seat.
- I am a seat belt.
- I am a handbrake.
- We are... a car!

See if players can vary the pace of the game, sometimes playing with just a few people and sometimes employing the whole group. Players have to observe each other, listen, and take a collective breath when they feel it's time to speak in one voice. They are working in agreement and committing at each stage of the game.

When an offer is made, it either suggests, or sits within, what Keith Johnstone refers to as a 'circle of ideas' or 'expectation'.[10] In the early days of training, keep the ideas within the circle, rather than trying to be original and coming up with anarchic suggestions.

For example, if the first offer is 'I am a planet', there is a circle of expectation around 'planet' – stars, suns, moons, rockets, black holes, asteroids, satellites, etc. It's also easy to identify anything *outside* this circle – tax returns, doll houses, soufflés, garden furniture, etc.

Each offer narrows and tightens the circle as suggestions become more closely related.

If the opening offer is 'I am a sofa', it might suggest a living room, and players could add other items of furniture. But if the second player were to say 'I am a junkyard', then the circle of expectation shifts focus. We might now imagine the sofa as being discarded in a junkyard and explore ideas from that world instead.

'I am a wall' is a very open suggestion that may occupy several different circles of expectation. We might be part of a castle, a

10. Keith Johnstone, *Impro for Storytellers*, Faber and Faber, 1999, pp. 79–80.

boundary between nations, a prison yard, a dry stone wall in the countryside, a house, an office partition, etc.

With each subsequent suggestion the circle tightens until the context becomes more clearly defined. If the second person were to join with the offer 'I am Emperor Hadrian', it would suggest the context of Hadrian's Wall.

This is how most improvisation works. By building one step at a time, the bigger picture is revealed.

Making obvious and connected choices is a good place to start. And if players seem tense, fearful and stuck, remind them they can copy offers already made in the scene.

'I am a tree' can be joined by 'I am another tree' to create a forest, an orchard or a garden. In fact, my favourite version of this game was a LAMDA group that played as follows:

- I am a book.

- I am another book.

- I am another book.

- I am another book.

- I am also a book.

- I am another book.

- We are… books!

One Voice

The final part of the *Sandwiches* game requires the whole group to speak in unison. This exercise develops the idea and practice of speaking as one.

A group (I suggest starting with five or six people) stands together in a tight semicircle with their arms around each other, and talks as one person in one voice. I usually begin by explaining that I am going to interview them and that I will start by asking them their name, to which they must reply, in unison: 'My name is…' From that point on they are improvising.

With practice and encouragement, a group can speak quite quickly, though it's always good to coach them to go even faster. Ideally we shouldn't see one person leading the others very much – if at all. Players who have a tendency to lead will have to learn to follow, and those who tend to follow will have to step up and lead more.

It's a great exercise for practising the three basic principles: players have to attend to each other very closely (*listen*), immediately acknowledge whatever direction the group seems to be going in (*accept*), and play boldly (*commit*), otherwise the game falls apart. When performers let go of their fear of 'getting it wrong' and discover confidence and a playful spirit, the game becomes entertaining and surprising. It is even possible for players to commit to the beginning of a word without knowing what that word will be by its end.

To begin with, pose questions with relatively short answers:

- How old are you?
- Where are you from?
- What do you do for a living?

As the players gather confidence, you can push them into more complex interaction:

- What advice would you give someone wanting to enter your profession?
- What's the most embarrassing thing that ever happened to you?
- What's your life ambition?

I have seen groups singing songs, reciting poetry, talking in other languages… anything is possible.

You can play with any number of people (I've seen it played with two people and with over thirty).

Don't let them off the hook – if they don't make sense, challenge them to say a word again or explain why they just said what they said. Compelling them to make sense helps to improve their commitment to the exercise.

Tribes

Sometimes it's fun to play longer, more immersive improvisation games, and this is a good behavioural exercise for groups of ten players or more. I am grateful to Paul Abrahams for this game, originally created to get actors to engage with music in a playful, abstract manner.

The group is a tribe that communicates with sound and movement. For example, players might be a squat, crawling tribe who communicate with low, rhythmic, staccato grunts; or they may stand on tiptoes, speaking in high, sonorous tones, singing light, falling phrases. There is no need to agree on anything in advance – everything is discovered during play.

Players begin in a circle, asleep. After a minute or so they awaken and start to communicate, improvising in a whole new language of abstract gibberish, and exploring new ways of relating to one another. Maybe a status chain emerges, maybe they are all equal, maybe they sit and talk or engage in activities. Allow it to unfold at whatever pace seems to suit the group.

After a while, one of the tribe is selected to go on a quest to locate other tribes. They are blessed by their community in a ritual ceremony and sent on their way. The selected tribesperson leaves the room and the tribe goes back to sleep.

A few minutes later the envoy returns to the room and the tribe. They have been across the mountains, encountered a new tribe, and have learned a whole new language and method of communication, contrasting to their present one. The envoy teaches everyone in their tribe this new language until the tribe is transformed.

After some time, a new envoy is selected to go and find another tribe. And so on, with new envoys finding new tribes and bringing back new languages for as long as you wish.

The game seems to work best lasting around thirty to forty-five minutes, with five or six envoys going and returning in that time.

There are very few guidelines for this game. It's designed to allow actors to explore musicality, but is also an effective behavioural exercise for status, joining, gibberish, tempo and emotional change – all terms that will be examined in more detail later. Although it can provoke some extreme behaviour, the lack of a single point of focus or exposure allows players to immerse themselves for a longer period of time, and it will generate a number of interesting points for discussion afterwards.

On Tension, Relaxation and Flow

There are tensions integral to improvising that can be entertaining. Audiences enjoy seeing players 'put on the spot', thinking and reacting under pressure. They also enjoy experiencing the tensions created during spontaneous narrative construction. Observing improvisers communicate their ideas with one another to build a story can be like watching a group of people putting up a tent in a storm – the challenge can be thrilling. But there are forms of tension unhelpful to the performer and alienating to the audience (the tension that arises from insecurity, incompetence or poor communication, for example). Unnecessary tension impairs effective observation and listening.

I once hosted a workshop for Torontonian Becky Johnson, who, for almost a whole hour, coached people simply to look at each other – *genuinely* look at each other – and, moreover, allow themselves *to be seen*, free from forced scrutiny or our protective masks. It took a long time for the participants to relax enough and release some of their awkwardness and self-consciousness, but the connection between performers in the scenes they played subsequently was magical. Anything encouraging players to alleviate unnecessary tension is useful, and there are dozens of icebreakers and drama games you can call upon. Remember, though, some games and exercises actually cause tension, especially when the player is 'trying to get it right' or becomes self-conscious for any reason. I have seen simple exercises explained with such a lack of clarity that scowls of concentration begin to appear on the players' faces before they have even started. Find what works for you and your group. Keep it light. Do whatever makes it easier for people to allow themselves to be seen.

We rebel against whatever we are commanded to do. The worst thing someone can say to you when you are tense is 'Relax.' When did that ever work? Or tell you to 'cheer up' if you are depressed? If we could command our emotions as we please, we would presumably choose to be happy all the time. It's the same when told to 'get out of your head', and it is the same with tension.

Some forms of tension are necessary. Acting teacher Yat Malmgren promoted a study of acting based around levels and states of tension. But the unnecessary and unwanted tension of the improviser is problematic because it distances the audience from their desire and ability to engage with the action.

It is possible for a performer to observe tension in their body and consciously release it, but this takes study and practice. The easiest solution, as always, is to focus outwardly. As the performer becomes less self-conscious, the unwanted tension dissipates.

Creativity and Imagination

Actors often talk about how the lines in the script do all the work for them. In fact, many artists say that when their artistic process is in full flow, it doesn't feel like creating so much as *channelling*.

I have found that with my best work – as a performer, writer or composer – it often feels like I am not doing very much, I'm just… *there*. In improvisation we often think we have to come up with good ideas to create the entertainment, which is certainly true sometimes. During a show there are occasions when you are required to steer the action using your craft. But at its best, all the beats of the scenes are passing through you, and innovation is a surprise, not a goal. In script-based performance, emotion is best discovered as a by-product of *intention*. When the actor focuses outwardly and attempts to initiate change in others, they will find that something happens to themselves as a result.

If you have seen a quick-witted, wordy improviser dazzling the audience with impressive speed and vocabulary, it's easy to think you have to be the same. It's intimidating or inspiring, depending upon your outlook. Attempting to replicate such things is likely to cause tension and unhappiness. Just as improvisers experience a pressure to be interesting, they will also experience a pressure to be creative.

Instead, let creativity flow. To do this you need be present – place your focus on a target outside yourself, and engage with the situation moment by moment as it unfolds. Truthful behaviour will always sustain our interest and attention so long as the scene is moving forward. There will be days when the words will come and others when they don't. Some people are innately wordier than others, just as some are naturally funny, brave, shy or witty. Creativity may be compelled under pressure but it can also flow from relaxation. Everyone has an equal capacity for creativity and imagination. Maximising one's potential is about identifying obstacles and employing techniques to remove them. Above all, don't tell yourself you aren't creative or imaginative. It simply isn't true.

'No, That's Not It'

Player A begins by performing an activity and player B joins. They relate to each other in any way they wish, with or without dialogue. The content isn't important, all that matters is the connection being made. At some point, B will comment on the activity ('Well, looks like we got all the weeds up now'), to which A, who might usually respond with 'Yes, and…' will instead reply:

'No, that's not it' and begin to do something else. B will observe once more and then join in as before. Whenever B comments on the activity, A says: 'No, that's not it' and starts something new. Don't start a new scene or change the characters, just switch the activity. B can't get tense about the concept of making a mistake because *everything they do will be wrong*. They must get used to releasing the tensions caused by their attachment to outcome and moving on with whatever is happening in the scene.

A note on failure

Failure of any kind hurts. For those who enjoy improv as a hobby, there has often been a desire to pretend failure doesn't exist, to keep the hobby joyful.

It all depends why you are doing improv, of course, but I never learned anything of real value that didn't come with a few bruises. Failure is always an opportunity for learning.

Still Waxing On And Off

When working with a new group I will spend as much time as possible employing games to encourage playfulness and freedom of expression, cultivating an environment free from traditional notions of right and wrong. I will also employ non-verbal exercises so that players don't worry about generating content. (In improv terms, *content* is basically what you say. Games in which everyone is speaking at the same time and there is no single point of focus can allow novices to feel relaxed and playful. Exposing them in front of the whole group can be intimidating and make the improviser self-conscious about what they are doing and saying.)

When you feel the time is right to add language and content, try starting with some of Keith Johnstone's storytelling games.

Story One-Word-at-a-Time

Two players, alternating words, tell a story.

Start simply, with the phrase: 'Once upon a time...'

It's great training for keeping people connected and in the moment. As in the game *Sandwiches*, players are encouraged to say the next *obvious and connected* word, otherwise the performance quickly falters.

Things to look out for

Wimping

-   Once upon a time there was a – big – large – giant – big – massive...

Neither player will commit to the noun. They are usually afraid of saying something uninteresting or revealing. Go there! Say anything. 'Once upon a time there was a... cat.' Fine. There are plenty of good stories about cats. Besides, learning how to sustain interest is something we will look at later. For now, the obvious, instinctive choice is a good starting point.

Endgaming

Players often race ahead, trying to force the sentence where they want it to go. Remind players that they cannot control the story, neither its content nor its destination. Responsibility is shared.

Of course, it is difficult *not* to suddenly imagine where the sentence, or indeed the whole story, might end up, but players must be able to relinquish attachment to any of their ideas, making this game good training for being in the moment while having an eye on the future – a concept that will repeatedly appear in later sections about improvising longer narratives.

Emotional change

Varying the emotional content helps sustain an audience's attention and interest. Some players bark out the words robotically because they are tense and attempting to maintain control, or at least trying not to make mistakes. Remind them that they cannot make mistakes and that they are not in control of the whole exercise. Change the emotional tone – imagine you are playing a stage direction as you might have in a script, leading you towards a different emotional choice. This new tone can be established in a single word. For example:

- (*Mysteriously.*) 'Suddenly...'
- (*Wondrously.*) 'Amazingly...'
- (*Sadly.*) 'However...'

The player does not have to know where the story is going in order to commit to a new emotion. In fact, the change of emotion subsequently shapes the story.

It is also easier to follow and build on a scene partner's emotional change than try to generate content mechanically.

Sense

Don't worry if the story doesn't make sense. Incorporate all errors and mistakes and they will cease to be errors and mistakes. Or start again.

Remind the players that if the story isn't going where you thought it would go, let go of your initial ideas. Get used to practising this kind of *immediate yield*. Play with complete commitment to process and no attachment to the outcome. In *Showstopper!* we often say: 'Play the story that is emerging, not the story you think it should have been.'

Variants

There are numerous variants on one-word-at-a-time story games. You can have any number of players. I've seen Canadian company

Rapid Fire Theatre delight a crowd by playing with two rows of improvisers tagging each other in and out at frantic speed.

I encourage some groups to assign someone who can write or type quickly to transcribe a one-word-at-a-time story played with a large team and lasting an hour or more. Read back the results afterwards for some fascinating and surreally entertaining insights into the collective unconscious.

Story One-Sentence-at-a-Time

Two players – A and B – sit facing each other a comfortable distance apart.

A begins to tell a story to B, one sentence (or rather a thought, a beat or part of a sentence) at a time. If B likes the offer, they say 'Yes' and A progresses with the next sentence. If B says 'No' then A must come up with a different sentence until B accepts it, at which point they may again progress.

A. Once upon a time there was a knight.

B. Yes.

A. Who was the bravest in all the land.

B. No.

A. Who was a complete coward.

B. Yes.

A. And one day he was commanded to slay a dragon.

B. Yes.

A. But he refused.

B. No.

A. So he accepted.

B. Yes.

A. And, in the forest, drawing closer to the dragon's cave, he became more terrified than ever before.

B. Yes.

A. So he ran away.

B. No.

A. So he hid in the bushes.

B. No.

A. He sat down to have lunch.

B. No.

A. He sent his servant into the cave instead.

B. No.

A. Quaking with fear, he went into the cave anyway.

B. Yes!

As you will see, in this game, B is really the storyteller, and A is channelling the story they think B wishes to hear. In the above example, B liked the idea of a cowardly knight having to do something dangerous, and didn't want A to let the knight get out of trouble so easily.

Whenever A receives a 'No' from B, you will notice the tendency is for player A to look away, to flick their eyes up or down into a 'processing/thinking' space in order to come up with a new idea. This is a moment of disconnection. It's at this point that A's attention should be drawn back to B, back into connection with the other player. I often coach player As by saying: 'Pretend you can read B's mind. Study their face for clues about how they might be feeling or what they might be thinking.'

It's also a good exercise for working with *yes* and *no* and showing that both are important parts of scenework and storytelling.

Another version

Play with a group of approximately five people in a circle.

This begins as a one-word-at-a-time story, moving around the circle. The second time around the circle, each player uses two words, then three words on the third time around, then four, then three again, then two again, finally ending with a circuit of single words.

Freeform Give-and-Take

Have a group of five or six people tell a story in which individuals can speak for as long as they wish before someone else intervenes and continues. As soon as someone takes over the story, the original teller yields and stops talking. Try to vary the frequency of interruption as much as possible – a player might talk for a full minute or only say three words before someone else takes over. There should be no fixed sequence, pattern or order as to who speaks when.

One On, One Off

Also known as 'Gravid Water', this game is usually played with two performers – one reading dialogue from a script while the other is improvising. The first player must stick to the exact order of the lines as presented on the page. They may interpret these lines any way they wish but will inevitably be taking them out of the original context of the play. The player without a script must make strong endowments, offers and counteroffers, even though they have no idea what line their scene partner will be compelled to say next. Both must play boldly to make this game work, as much of the joy lies in how emerging reality-clashes affect the performers. Polite, cautious engagement will eliminate the elements of risk and will be less appealing both to play and to watch.

It can be played with any number of performers, but works best when only one of the group is off-book. Modern scripts with short lines tend to be most effective, but you can play it with any author, past or present. It is often a good way to get players improvising in the style of Shakespeare, for example.

Get Physical

The danger of too much wordy storytelling is that players lose awareness of their bodies and *think* their way through what to say next. You will observe bodies swaying, fidgeting, and eyes disconnecting from other players, as if searching the ceiling for answers. Instruct players to get physical. Encourage eye contact. Act out the story wherever possible. Go on the same adventure as the characters or even add abstract movement to each word. And remind players that not everything has to make sense. If they are spending too long looking for a word they can shout 'blank' or 'blah' or anything else to keep the story moving. If they get stuck they can start again whenever they want. Everything is ephemeral and players should enjoy the process rather than worry about the results. For now, commitment, agreement and collaboration are all that is important.

Players will get a feel for how powerful story can be. I usually let them build a story and then stop them after a few minutes. Sometimes people are frustrated because they desperately want to know what happens next. In one class at LAMDA a player refused to stop because they simply had to know how the story ended.

These story games will lay a foundation for the scene and story work we are now going on to examine. Revisit them often.

Summary

Listen

Listening is the willingness to be changed.

Accept

Work with each other's ideas.

Allow yourself to be affected by what's going on around you.

Commit

Be bold.

Try not to judge yourself, or what's happening. Engage with the moment playfully.

Observe Others

Work with what is already there.

Be curious and attentive.

Note the pressure to be interesting, funny or clever.

Don't be afraid to make simple, obvious, connected choices.

Outward focus is the key to all effective acting.

Let Go

Play without attachment to outcome.

Practise acting immediately upon impulse.

3.

The Scene

As we get used to working with each other's ideas, being affected by each other, and committing to what is happening in the here and now, we can begin to shape scenes.

A written scene can be divided into *units* and *beats*. Similarly, an improvised scene is created using little units of action called *offers*. When each offer relates to the previous one, a scene begins to unfold. The performers may not know where the scene is going or even what it is about at first, but with effective listening and connected offers, the content, themes and games all wondrously unfold. Del Close once said that improvising a scene was like building an aeroplane while it was in mid-flight.

There are numerous terms we need to understand, and several techniques to adopt. Here are some more tools for the toolkit.

Furthering, Advancing and Broadening

Group 'Yes'

Best played with a group of more than ten.

One person in the group suggests an activity:

– Let's go to the beach!

To which the whole group enthusiastically responds:

– Yes, let's!

And then, as a group, they pretend to go to a beach and do various activities until someone else in the group suggests the next step:

– Let's build a sandcastle.

To which the rest of the group responds once more with:

– 'Yes, let's!'

And then everyone engages in sandcastle-building activities. Until the next suggestion.

And so on.

However, there is an important caveat. If, at any point, any member of the group doesn't wish to engage with the suggested activity, for whatever reason, they drop out of the game and sit down. The game stops when half the group, or more, has left. The challenge is to see how long the group can collectively make the game last.

This is an exercise in *advancing* or *furthering*, keeping the suggestions connected so that they are sequential and one leads logically to the next. If players fragment and begin to *broaden* –

A. Let's go to the beach.

GROUP. Yes, let's!

A. Let's go to the moon.

GROUP. Yes, let's!

A. Let's do press-ups.

GROUP. Yes… okay, let's.

A. Let's all have a fight!

GROUP. Er…

– then members of the group will start to drop out very quickly and the game won't last long. When offers are connected and sequential, players are less likely to drop out.

A. Let's go to the magical forest.

GROUP. Yes, let's!

A. Let's go to the oldest tree in the forest.

GROUP. Yes, let's!

A. Let's go to the door in the trunk of the tree.

GROUP. Yes, let's!

A. Let's open the door.

GROUP. Yes, let's!

A. Let's step inside.

It is less likely that many players will have dropped out of this narrative because the units of action are sequential and connected. The players will want to know what happens next.

Groups soon learn that simple, playful offers engage others more effectively than offers of poor taste or aggression.

— Let's sneak into the haunted house.

– is usually more appealing than –

— Let's drink too much and throw up.

Distasteful, aggressive and subversive suggestions come up more than you might think, especially with beginners.

In a session led by improv veteran Ben Benison, I volunteered to play a scene with him. He noticed that I had my arms folded and said: 'The first thing I want you to do is to adopt an attitude that makes me think you want to play with me.'

Seek to create games that others wish to play.

Later we will look at when *broadening* is useful, but for now let's focus on *advancing* and *furthering*.

'What Happens Next?'

One player (A) stands in front of a panel of three (B, C and D).

A asks: 'What happens first?'

One of the panellists will respond by giving a simple instruction, such as: 'You look down at the floor' or 'You are doing the washing-up.'

Actor A then carries out the instruction. It can be carried out in any way the actor chooses, but in the early days of training I would encourage the actor to be relatively uninflected, i.e. not to add too much and to perform the instruction simply.

A then asks: 'What happens next?'

And a different panellist will give the next instruction, and so on.

Panellists are not allowed to speak twice consecutively. This shares out the instructions and prevents any one contributor from controlling the story.

Just as with one-word-at-a time-story exercises, players cannot dominate each other and must learn to yield.

Players should seek to advance or further what is already happening, rather than broaden out into contrasting or conflicting ideas. It takes some practice. *Broadening* results in exchanges like this:

A. What happens first?

B. You are doing the washing-up.

   A *does so for a while and then, still washing up, asks:*

A. What happens next?

D. You hear a gunshot outside.

   A *reacts as if listening, with a sense of alarm.*

A. What happens next?

C. Your telephone rings.

> A, *already getting confused by the disconnected elements, gets out their phone.*

A. What happens next?

B. An alien spacecraft lands.

> A, *looking out of a window, awkwardly forcing a sense of amazement.*

A. What happens next?

D. You realise it isn't a spaceship.

The players have moved a long way from a character washing up, and the storytellers are broadening multiple ideas rather than unifying and furthering one idea. They even start negating some of their ideas ('A spaceship lands' – 'No, actually it's not a spaceship'). And they are desperately trying to be interesting.

Furthering or *advancing* the scene might look like this:

A. What happens first?

B. You are doing the washing-up.

> A *does so for a while and then, still washing up, asks*:

A. What happens next?

C. You notice something in the water.

A. What happens next?

D. You reach into the water.

A. What happens next?

B. You pull out your wedding ring.

A. What happens next?

D. You are relieved you didn't lose it.

A. What happens next?

C. You put it back on your finger.

A. What happens next?

D. You carry on with the washing-up.

A. What happens next?

B. You notice something else in the water...

Here we are employing *agreement* with each other's offers, *pattern recognition, reincorporation* and *advancing* one idea.

First-time players reveal negative and/or destructive tendencies very quickly:

A. What happens first?

B. You are dancing.

A. What happens next?

C. You fall over and break your leg.

Or:

A. What happens first?

C. You take a slice of your birthday cake.

A. What happens next?

D. It's mouldy.

The negative impulse seems interesting to the player, but it is, in fact, drawn from a need for safety and, in most cases, it closes down avenues of development. Novices, uncertain to trust being in the moment, undermine it.

Coach players to make positive, connected, obvious choices and sustain them for as long as possible. Choices do not always have to be positive in improv, but habitual negativity is tiring. This is something worth addressing early in training.

Make sure the panellists are observing actor A and paying attention to the way A is asking for and carrying out instructions. There is usually plenty of information in A's behaviour to make the next choice obvious for the panel too. If actor A asks: 'What happens first?' and appears open, relaxed and happy, then a *dark* first offer is outside our circle of expected ideas. Build on what you see.

A (*smiling, restlessly*). What happens first?

B. You are dancing.

A *does so with great joy and vigour.*

A. What happens next?

D. You pull off some amazing moves.

Panellists will often attempt to be funny, interesting, unusual and sometimes downright weird.

Students will often ask: 'But what's wrong with being surreal or unusual? What's wrong with being unexpected or surprising?'

Of course, *nothing* is wrong with this, but let's learn how to draw like da Vinci before we paint like Picasso.

Remember McKee? 'Anxious, inexperienced writers obey rules. Rebellious, unschooled writers break rules. Artists master the form.'

It can be a challenge to keep the offers connected. Players, fearful of being boring, can lose faith very quickly. Repeated practice can help players remain confident in their offers while maintaining sequence and connection.

Two other techniques to explore in this game:

Pattern Recognition

and

Reincorporation

If a panellist breaks the furthering of the scene and jumps to a new idea, coming back to the original idea can be very satisfying. After all, why show anything if it is quickly abandoned in favour of something else? For example:

A. What happens first?

B. You are brushing your teeth.

A. What happens next?

C (*noticing that A is doing it very slowly and carefully*). You lean in towards the mirror as you methodically clean every tooth.

A (*doing so, taking the direction effectively*). What happens next?

D. You start to shave.

The players have abandoned the meticulous brushing of teeth and broadened to shaving.

D might argue that the offer 'you start to shave' is within the world of 'ablutions in a bathroom', but the furthering of *carefully and methodically brushing one's teeth* has been dropped. This is a small distinction but an important one. A pattern has been broken and another (albeit related) has begun.

In this case, we won't mind so long as A's 'careful, methodical' behaviour is maintained or brought back. We might even go back to brushing teeth again later in the game, and by doing so may discover A to be obsessive in some way.

The panel of instructors will often find it difficult to further one single idea and consequently the scene may split into two strands of action.

A. What happens first?

C. You are reaching for something up high.

A. What happens next?

D. You stretch your fingertips but can't quite get it.

A. What happens next?

C. You stand on tiptoe but still can't reach it.

A. What happens next?

B. You look around for a chair.

A. What happens next?

D. You find a chair.

A. What happens next?

B. You place the chair where you need it.

A. What happens next?

C. You hear a sound behind you.

The 'sound' offer no longer furthers the notion of 'trying to reach something' – it is instead a broadening of ideas in the scene. The performers now have two strands of action. This needn't be a problem so long as they continue to look for connection between the strands.

A. What happens next?

D. You look around.

A. What happens next?

B. You see your brother is laughing at you.

A. What happens next?

C. You ignore him and climb up on the chair.

A. What happens next?

B. You finally reach the football on the roof of the garage and pick it up.

A. What happens next?

D. You throw it at your brother!

Here the two strands of action are:

- Reaching for something (which turns out to be a football).

- Your brother laughing at you.

Note that the two idea came together quite well. In fact, the players might not have had any idea what the actor was reaching for until the laughing brother was added, suggesting all sorts of possible contexts for the scene.

Reincorporation of the original ideas is essential, although you may be surprised to discover how far one single idea can be developed. Furthermore, audiences enjoy seeing players reincorporate in scenes and stories. The longer the gap between the initial idea and its reincorporation, the more satisfying the bringing back of the idea becomes.

Each time there is a disconnection from furthering/advancing, a new strand of action will appear. When this happens, regard each idea as a new ball being juggled. So long as they all remain in the air, the juggler can continue. But to *replace* one idea with another, abandoning the original idea altogether, will inevitably lead the audience to ask: 'Why did they do that in the first place if they were never going to return to it?' If the above scene developed into a sibling argument and we never discovered what the actor was reaching for, we would be left with a feeling of incompletion.

Audiences, in the main, infer connections and conclusions and will add their own if none are provided by the players.

There is a sequence in Mel Brooks' comedy *The Producers* that perfectly illustrates how a broadening of multiple ideas can all be drawn into the advancing of one main idea. When Leo Bloom becomes hysterical, Max Bialystock throws a glass of water in his face to calm him down. After a momentary shock, Bloom starts complaining about being hysterical and wet. When a desperate Bialystock slaps him, Bloom realises he is in pain, as well as being wet and still being hysterical.

The disciplines in *What Happens Next?* are akin to scales for the piano – an essential part of training for improvising scenes, facilitating the practice and understanding of:

- Furthering.
- Advancing one beat at a time (and keeping each beat connected).
- Letting go of attachment to ideas and outcome (yield).
- Recognising and releasing tendencies to dominate and control.
- Working with what is already there.
- Developing faith in your offers.
- Working with other players' offers.
- Uninflected action.

- Create nothing – invent nothing.
- Pattern recognition.
- Reincorporation.

Invisibility Game

This exercise requires a few sturdy props that may end up being thrown around.

Player A and player B share the same space, but A is invisible to B and B is invisible to A. The game is best played without dialogue – the setting of late evening in a library tends to suit well.

A and B can hear each other and, should either of them pick up a prop, the other would see it as if it were floating in the air.

Play for a few minutes, allowing the characters to respond, investigate, and slowly discover each other in the library.

There are many things I like about this game. It encourages people to slow down and give full meaning and significance to each beat. If A is sitting reading a book and suddenly sees B's bag floating across the room (as B shoulders it and moves over to another stack) then it will take A time to process this unusual occurrence. Is it scary? Is it intriguing? Do they think they are going mad? Are their eyes playing tricks on them? Will they get up to investigate? It will be obvious when the players are rushing through the beats, not allowing themselves full processing time. When both players allow the beats to affect them it can be enthralling and hilarious to watch.

You can develop the game as a clown exercise. Each time a new beat occurs, which a performer has to process, they 'check in' with the audience. Can the audience see this too? What do they make of this situation? Players, in turn, respond to how the audience reacts.

New Choice

Play a scene and, whenever you ring the bell, the player who last made an offer must erase their offer and immediately come up with something else instead – a new choice. It's useful, and usually very enjoyable, to force the player into numerous new choices in a row. Let the players establish a scene for a while and then start to interrupt with the bell.

 — Let's go for a ride.

   Ding! New choice.

 — Let's go shopping.

   Ding! New choice.

 — Let's climb a mountain.

   Ding! New choice.

 — Let's stay right here.

   Ding! New choice.

 — I always wanted to be a singer.

   Ding! New choice.

 — I feel so alone.

   Ding! New choice.

 — I'm in love with you.

And as no further new choice is compelled by the bell, the scene continues from: 'I'm in love with you.'

This is a powerful exercise to help players give up their attachment to any imagined outcome.

Forward Movement

A scene is like a shark. It must keep moving forward, otherwise it dies.

It can move forward slowly or it can move forward quickly, but it must progress and develop. Even Samuel Beckett's

Waiting for Godot (described as a play in which 'nothing happens, twice') has progression and development. The audience, in any drama, is primarily interested in *what happens next*, be it a breathtaking plot twist or a simple human interaction.

The most common way to prevent a scene from moving forward is for the performers to start arguing. Too many players feel this is interesting to audiences, perhaps because they have often been taught that *all drama is conflict*.

A. Let's play tennis.

B. I don't want to play tennis.

A. You never want to play tennis.

B. What's that supposed to mean?

A. Forget it.

B. Do you want to play or not?

A. I don't care.

B. Why do you always do this?

A. Do what?

B. You know what.

A. Shut up.

The above dialogue might play effectively when scripted and rehearsed, but in improvisation the audience quickly becomes aware that the performers have not found agreement, causing unease.

There are numerous ways to prevent a scene from progressing.

Negation

To oppose and thereby cancel or reverse an offer:

  A. Let's go to the beach.

  B. No, let's go to the pub.

B has accepted A's offer of going somewhere, but it would be much more effective to accept A's offer fully and simply go to the beach. It's usually a performer's need to maintain control that causes negation.

Resistance

To be unwilling to follow instruction or invitation:

  A. Let's go to the beach.

  B. I don't want to go to the beach.

Are we going to have an argument? Will it be interesting to watch? Or shall we just accept and move forward?

Jill Bernard elegantly illustrates resistance in her *Small Cute Book of Improv*[11] with an example scene of a teenage girl being compelled to go to a fancy-dress party by her parents. She rails against it, she complains, she says that it's embarrassing, all the while putting on the ridiculous costume and clambering into the car. Here, resistance is a detail of her *character* and the cause of *personal conflict*, but the scene continues with *forward movement*. Despite her protests, she is going to the party. The characters may be arguing, but the actors are in agreement.

Similar problems can arise with characters that are drunk or under the influence of drugs, or the very young and the very elderly. A child throwing a tantrum may seem 'in character', but it often delays or destroys a scene's progress. A character's

---

11. Jill Bernard, *Jill Bernard's Small Cute Book of Improv*, Yesand.com publishing.

condition, emotion or belief can easily prevent the forward movement of the scene.

Resisting can occur in useful ways, for example by creating or exploiting dramatic tension:

    A. Cut the green wire.

    B. Wait. I don't know...

    A. The green! Come on, we don't have time.

    B. It's not the green. Let me think about this –

    A. They're coming – cut it – now!

But it can also reveal a fear of engaging with something surprising or dangerous:

    A. Are you having an affair?

    B. What makes you say that?

    A. Are you?

    B. I don't want to have this conversation.

Blocking

To deny or shut down the reality of the offer:

    A. Let's go to the beach.

    B. What beach? I don't know you.

I try not to use the word 'blocking' when teaching because students can get very hung up on it. In fact, the more it is discussed, the more it prevails. However, it is such a ubiquitous term that we need to be aware of it. Blocking is most easily avoided if the performer is focusing on something to do rather than worrying about something to avoid.

Glibness

To lower the emotional stakes in the original offer:

    A. Your house is on fire!

    B (*shrugs*). It's okay – it always does that.

Or glibness on behalf of someone else:

    A. This is it, I'm dying.

    B. No, you're not. There. I have just saved you.

Emotion, scene development and character are *all* negated here.

Emotional vulnerability and truthful behaviour can be challenging for the novice in front of an audience. As a result, glibness is very common. It often elicits a laugh from the audience, but it comes at the expense of developing the scene, and will certainly impact development beyond the scene. Glibness masks fear and insecurity.

Meisner, quoting George Bernard Shaw, reminds us that 'Self-betrayal, magnified to suit the optics of the theatre, is the whole art of acting.'[12]

Self-betrayal: the dropping of the protective mask.

Even the performer whose primary aim is to be funny sometimes forgets that emotionally truthful behaviour makes them funnier. Of all the ways to avoid the wonders of improvisation, glibness is the worst. It lowers standards, diminishes expectations, destroys development of ideas, and is disrespectful to your scene partners.

---

12. Sanford Meisner and Dennis Longwell, *Sanford Meisner on Acting*, Vintage, 1987, p. 145.

Bridging/Delaying

To create unnecessary delay in getting on with the offer:

   A. Let's go to the beach.

   B. I can't go yet.

Or:

   A. Let's play tennis.

   B. Wait. I've lost my racket. I can't find my racket.

Again, this is a method of control, to avoid moving forward into the unknown.

The only reason to deliberately delay moving a scene forward is if the performers have discovered an entertaining option – a game, or a clown routine (what *Commedia dell'Arte* players used to call a *lazzo*), for example.

Keith Johnstone would play an exercise with students in which he instructed a couple of them to climb aboard an imaginary boat and row to an island. Oh, so many dramas happened in that boat! Fighting, arguing, murder, love, you name it. *But Johnstone observed that nobody would ever get to the island.* While we may not care about this if the scene in the boat is compelling, we should note that the objective is not being met. Arguing in the boat detains the players safely in the world of the *known*. Forward movement of a scene, by necessity, will take performers onto the island of the *unknown*.

Consider:

   A. Are you having an affair?

   B. No.

I have seen the 'Are you having an affair?' scene a thousand times and almost every single time, character B will say 'No', even if they have been trained to say 'Yes'. However, players often say 'No' in such a way as to let the audience know that they are hiding something, that they probably *are* having an affair but aren't confessing it. This scene inevitably becomes an argument, with A accusing and B denying, and while that can work fine, consider:

A. Are you having an affair?

B. Yes.

Now the scene is exciting and dangerous. Something is changing. The ensuing argument will have a very different emotional tone. The characters and the actors are deep in trouble.

Saying 'No' in the first instance is a natural response, and a sensitivity to drama may allow development of some subtext in the scene, but the audience will likely be more excited by the 'Yes' version.

Arguing, bridging, delaying, blocking, negating and resisting are seldom enjoyable to watch, even though all should be part of the improviser's skillset, ready to be used when required. Yes, even glibness.

When might these things be required?

In narrative improvisation, if the plot is moving too fast, with too many players attempting to create too much story, or there hasn't been enough time for events to impact the characters, then you may well need to *delay* or *resist*. A character under the influence of drink or drugs might use *blocking* to demonstrate that their perception of reality is different from others'. And if there is so much going on that the actor is being bombarded with numerous conflicting emotional offers and afforded little space in which to react, maybe *glibness* can actually help. We will look at all of this in more detail later when we discuss story.

Endowment

If you walk into a scene with me and call me 'Dad', you have just *endowed* me as being your father.

Endowment is attributing other players with identities or characteristics.

When you call me 'Dad', I discover, *at exactly the same time as the audience*, that I am playing your father. It's one of the joys of improvisation for performers and audiences alike.

You could endow me with a *relationship*: father, mother, family member, a friend, stranger, neighbour, work colleague, etc.

You could endow me with a *characteristic*: happy, sad, intelligent, oversensitive, drunk, etc.

You could endow me with a particular age, nationality or creed.

You could endow me as being a monster or a disembodied spirit, a gunslinger, a pirate, a police detective...

You can endow me as being... well, anything really.

- You're the best lawyer I know.

- I don't mean to be rude, Dad, but you're kind of clumsy. I'd rather put up those shelves myself.

- Don't be scared, Mitchell. You're the captain of this hockey team and all the boys of the St Aloysius First Eleven are right behind you!

You can endow the space around you, you can endow objects, you can endow pretty much anything. It is one of the most important tools in the improviser's kit.

Novice improvisers are often afraid to make clear, strong endowments. They worry that somehow they will get it wrong, or that their scene partner might not like their offer. This fear of upsetting fellow performers often inhibits the improviser, but in most cases your fellow performers will thank you for the endowment. It's a relief to have clarity in a scene without having to generate anything for oneself.

Remember – *there's no such thing as a mistake.*

Gifts

Players stand in a circle.

One player turns to the person next to them and hands over a gift.

The gift is mimed/imagined.

The recipient thanks the gift-giver and names the gift.

For example:

- A set of golf clubs. Great. Thanks.

Or:

- Thank you so much for this harpsichord.

The recipient then puts the gift to one side, reaches for a new gift and offers it to the next person in the circle, who names it (and so on).

Things to look out for

Novice players often tend towards the negative. They endow the gifts as being worthless or unpleasant and will seldom be happy to receive the gift at all.

- A lump of coal. Why did you get me this? (*Throws it over shoulder.*)

Most negativity in improvisation is defensive. By dismissing the importance of something, the improviser is protecting themselves from failure and judgement.

A. I've been thinking about this for some time. I think we should break up.

B. I wasn't in to this relationship anyway.

Or:

    A. You were ten seconds slower than last week!

    B. I don't really consider myself an athlete.

Improvising longform and narrative drama requires an understanding of what should matter, and when.

Spend time observing and noting how gifts are given and how they are received. Encourage the recipient to name the first thing they think of, as suggested by the size of the mimed object and how it is handled.

- How small is it?

- Was it handled with care?

- How hot is it?

- Is it solid or squidgy?

Encourage participants to commit to the mime; explore the size, weight and texture of the gift.

After a while you may wish to develop the game so that the receiver must accept their gift with a positive reaction and consequence.

    – A lump of coal. Amazing! I can light a fire.

    – A lump of coal. Wonderful. It can be the other eye
       for my snowman.

    – A lump of coal. Excellent! I'll take it to the lab and
       compress it into a diamond!

Positivity encourages the performer to move beyond knee-jerk defensiveness.

Remind the participant that they don't need to think up anything imaginative, amusing or impressive. It's more important to allow the gift to be emotionally affecting.

Watch out for players who plan their responses in advance. If the gift offered was held between thumb and forefinger and the recipient endows it as a rhino, they were most likely thinking ahead, or trying to subvert the game to be amusing. Thinking ahead and planning what to say can distance the performer from the immediacy of the moment. You can see the player's eyes glaze over when they are figuring out their response in advance. They are absenting themselves from the moment in order to think ahead. This is prevented when the recipient places their attention on the gift-giver and develops the trust to respond simply and truthfully in the moment.

This game flexes a couple of improv muscles:

1. *Endowment*: The recipient endows the gift by naming it. The giver nods and accepts that the gift has been correctly named. Even if they had a different idea at the time, they will yield.

2. *Emotional timbre*: After a while the gifts will develop meaning and significance. The recipient will be affected and changed by the gift.

You can use this exercise as a way into playing scenes, starting with the giving of a gift and then exploring the emotional response to it. Investing emotionally in the gift will make it easier to discover what the scene is about.

Common Psychosis

A game well suited to beginners, for up to fifteen players – although it works with players at any level of experience.

Arrange a semicircle of chairs, with one chair facing the whole group. Designate one player to be the 'psychiatrist' and ask them to leave the room.

The group now agrees on a 'common psychosis', some kind of quirk they all share. It can be behavioural, physical, verbal or psychological, but it must be something that everyone has in common, i.e. all players share the same endowment.

For example:

• The group is afraid to use words with the letter 'L' in them.

- The group believes that people with blue eyes are superior.

- The group is always looking for an opportunity to commit the perfect murder.

- Group members think they are in a soap opera.

- Group members behave like the person sitting to their left.

- Group members never answer a question without looking at two other people first.

- The group believes the year to be 1968.

...and so on. It can be quite literally anything, so long as all the members of the group have the belief or behaviour in common.

Once the common psychosis is established, don't let the players discuss it. Discover everything through gameplay with instinctive responses to the endowment.

The psychiatrist is then brought back into the room and must ask a series of questions, conducting interviews with individuals and the group as a whole, in an attempt to discover what the common psychosis is.

You can play with a time limit (five to ten minutes), or until the psychiatrist guesses correctly.

It will demonstrate how much drama (and fun) you can get out of a single endowment.

I once saw a group at LAMDA play 'the group believes that people with blue eyes are superior' endowment, and develop it into a full-blown revolution with the non-blue-eyed participants overthrowing those who had become their oppressors.

Goading

Putting someone on the spot with a strong endowment is often known among improvisers as *pimping*. I'd like to suggest a term with less problematic associations – *goading*. Goading is encouraging someone to go further: 'You're a poet, aren't you? Tell us in rhyming couplets.' It's putting someone in trouble, making them perform a certain task, or compelling them to perform in a certain way.

There's a great deal of fun to be had with goading, but experience has taught me not to do it until you get to know the people you are playing with.

For Del Close, putting pressure on someone in this way contradicts the cooperative ensemble elements of improvised performance.

I spent some years with Ken Campbell working the 'goader–rhapsode' dynamic, in which a (usually single) goader sets challenges for improvisers (rhapsodes), encouraging them to be increasingly daring. This model is used in *Showstopper!*, and some other companies I have worked with use it too.

Using Endowment in Scene-building

There are numerous ways to approach endowment when building a scene.

Let's focus on two of them – the 'immediate' and the 'organic'. Neither technique is necessarily *better* than the other. They are both useful in different situations.

1. Immediate endowment

Del Close trained his improvisers to master 'three-line initiations', in which the 'who, where and what' of the scene were created in the first three verbal exchanges.

For example:

> A. Professor Jenkins, it's gone midnight, what are you doing in the museum?

B. Sarah. I might have known my most conscientious student would still be here.

A. Need some help with those fossil samples?

As you can see, these offers are all *endowments*:

- Identity and relationship (Professor Jenkins and his student Sarah).
- Characteristics (Sarah is his 'most conscientious' student).
- Location (the museum).
- Time (gone midnight).
- Something specific and relevant in the space with them (fossil samples).

'The who, the where and the what' is often referred to as a 'platform'.

To start with, I suggest players only focus on the 'who' and the 'where'.

Who are these people and where is this scene taking place?

The 'what' is essentially asking the question: 'What is this scene about?' or 'What is the premise of the scene?'

In many ways the 'what' will look after itself, or at least emerge very quickly. In the above scene the endowment of identity, relationship, location and activity are all verbal endowments, but the performers' *behaviour* might provide clues as to what's really going on:

A (*startled*). Professor Jenkins, it's gone midnight, what are you doing in the museum?

B (*suspicious*). Sarah. I might have known my most conscientious student would still be here.

A (*trying to be friendly*). Need some help with those fossil samples?

Their behaviour provokes questions, not just in the minds of the audience but for the players too. There is a suggestion that one or both of them is hiding something, maybe doing something they shouldn't. The endowment of time ('gone midnight') feels a little sinister. Sarah certainly didn't expect to see her professor in the museum this late and the professor might, in turn, suspect her motives. Exploring this will uncover the 'what' of the scene.

Also consider:

> A (*fascinated*). Professor Jenkins, it's gone midnight, what are you doing in the museum?
>
> B (*relieved*). Sarah. I might have known my most conscientious student would still be here.
>
> A (*flirtatious*). Need some help with those fossil samples?

The 'who' and the 'where' are the same but the 'what' is now very different.

There is no need to agonise over identifying the 'what' of the scene. It's all contained in the behaviour of the opening exchanges:

> A (*confrontational*). Professor Jenkins, it's gone midnight, what are you doing in the museum?
>
> B (*evasive*). Sarah. I might have known my most conscientious student would still be here.
>
> A (*placatory*). Need some help with those fossil samples?

The 'who' and the 'where' are the same but the 'what' has changed.

Remember – endowment is not simply about what is said. Observation of behaviour is essential.

The ability to employ a three-line initiation swiftly can be very useful, sometimes essential. It can also create tension for the performer. The pressure to deliver something immediately can make less practised improvisers fluster and panic (and, indeed, practised ones too). The important thing is for the improviser to focus outwardly, directing attention to the other player(s), to observe and comment upon the obvious.

Time restrictions in shortform comedy generally encourage a quick, clear three-line initiation at the top of the scene, while longform and narrative improvisation often benefit from a more gradual development.

Benefits of *immediate* endowment:

- It provides clarity for performers and audiences.
- It facilitates faster progress and development.
- It gives the performers confidence quickly.

2. Organic endowment

When stepping into a scene, the performer should observe the other player's demeanour and behaviour.

If their shoulders are slumped and their eyes downcast, it may suggest they are sullen. So work with that: 'You seem sad' or 'You look depressed.' The novice improviser may ask their partner: 'You look sad – what's up?' but with more practice and confidence they can build the next step of the scene. They can *observe* that their scene partner is sad and *they can also assume that they know why*:

- You're better off without her, George.

Simply by observing, speculating and commenting on their partner's behaviour, an improviser unearths a lot of useful information. Their scene partner is sad, they have recently separated from someone, and they are a friend/colleague called George.

This doesn't have to be achieved solely through conversation/ dialogue. On observing my scene partner's sadness, I could react non-verbally and behave compassionately. I could lower my status to my partner, trying to cheer them up, or sit with them empathetically, a hand on their shoulder. My scene partner will then, in turn, play off this offer. And onwards we go. One beat at a time.

Benefits of *organic* endowment:

- Players allow the scene to unfold by being emotionally affected, rather than driving the scene from their 'writer's brain'.

- Often leads to more nuanced relationships, interactions and situations.

- Takes time pressure off the players.

'You Look...'

I developed this exercise after experimenting with elements of Sanford Meisner's work, adapting them to the requirements of improvising scenes.

Step one

Two players stand facing away from each other about six feet apart.

On the bell, turn and face each other.

Both players make a single observation in turn.

Start with the words 'You look...'

Speculate about the other person's mood. You don't have to be correct, you just have to say what you think you see.

- You look happy.

- You look nervous.

- You look like you are about to laugh.

When both A and B have spoken, they turn away, await the bell, and then repeat the exercise. Try this several times. Keep going until it is light, easy and immediate.

Step two

A makes the observation, B then accepts it:

> A. You look excited.
>
> B. I *am* excited.

Or:

> A. You look very pleased with yourself.
>
> B. I *am* very pleased with myself.

Play this repeatedly.

A is endowing B based upon whatever impulse arises when both players observe each other.

It doesn't matter if B wasn't actually feeling 'excited' or 'pleased with themselves'. They accept the offer and own the emotion made explicit.

Step three

Both players explore and advance the situation arising out of the observation.

> A. You look excited.
>
> B. I *am* excited.
>
> A. I can't believe we made it to the final.
>
> B. And we are going to win!

Or:

> A. You look very pleased with yourself.
>
> B. I *am* very pleased with myself.

A. Did you get the promotion?

B. I sure did.

Players can discover the 'what' of a scene very quickly. As they explore the situation, how they relate to one another will give clues as to their relationship and their environment (the 'who' and the 'where').

Step four

Use this exchange as a springboard into a scene.

Use *organic* endowment.

Maintain a truthful emotional connection based on observation. If at any stage either performer has a sense of who or where they are, they make it explicit.

Often a short scene will play out for a minute or two, and neither player has clearly endowed each other or the space they are in. They don't really know who they are or where they are and, as a result, the scene is hesitant. After the scene I often ask: 'Where did you *think* you were? Indoors or outdoors? Was it day or night? Open space or confined space?' The performers answer immediately and usually in agreement. Their instincts are articulated after the scene but remained unexpressed during it. It's the same with the relationship. Who are you to each other? Friends? Family? Lovers? Again, players usually have a good sense of this but fear to make it explicit in the scene. Repeat the exercise, encouraging them to make any instinctive ideas explicit.

For example:

A. You look excited.

B. I am excited, Jack.

> [A *has an impulse that the excitement could be due to it being* B*'s birthday. A explores this further.*]

A. Me too. Everyone's coming tonight.

> [*This in turn suggests an idea to* B.]

B. Really? Everyone's coming to my little leaving party?

[*So now the event has been made explicit. A immediately relinquishes the idea that it's B's birthday because B has now made it clear that it's their leaving party. Leaving what? Actor A has an instinct that it is about work and immediately voices it.*]

A. This office won't be the same without you, Katie.

[*We now know their working environment is an office. This offer is delivered sweetly, almost coyly. Maybe there is an attraction from A to B? Will B reciprocate?*]

B   (*suddenly more excited*). Is Steve coming?

[*A, observing B's excitement, has an instinct that B prefers Steve.*]

A. I guess so. (*Moves away, a little hurt.*) After all, he is our boss.

Note that, while verbal offers clarify specific endowments, important emotional and behavioural offers are being made at the same time.

In this brief exchange we have established the following:

- Jack and Katie are office colleagues.

- Tonight is Katie's leaving party and they are both excited about it.

- Jack has an attraction to Katie, which is expressed without much confidence.

- Katie is either oblivious to this attraction or ignoring it at present.

- Katie likes their boss, Steve, and this makes Jack a little hurt and jealous.

It takes longer to write out the situation than it does simply to play the scene.

It is also worth noting that, as the scene progressed, the performers let go of several ideas they had along the way. (A let go of the idea that it was B's birthday, for example.) You can't help but have ideas during a scene. It's natural. Treat ideas like balloons. Some will lift you into the air, others you can pop and let go of immediately.

There are still some unanswered questions:

- How long have they been working together?
- Why hasn't Jack told Katie how he really feels about her?
- Does Katie know about Jack's feelings?

We may wish to know more about the office.

- What kind of business is it?
- Where is tonight's party?

All these can be explored as the scene progresses.

Three-line initiations

A number of Canadian improvisers I know use the following template for three-line initiations:

Offer 1: Player A endows player B (relationship/identity).

Offer 2: Player B endows player A (relationship/identity) and endows the space (environment).

Offer 3: Move to activity.

For example:

> A (*offer 1*). Sister Murphy, I've set out all the garlands.
>
> B (*offer 2*). That's wonderful, Father Edwards, they make St Swithin's church look lovely.
>
> A (*offer 3*). Let me help you lay out the hymn books.

'Moving to activity' helps place the scene in its geographical context and encourages the players to invest in their environment. It also creates *staging*.

Assumed endowment

Sometimes, in order to move a scene forward, one of the performers can assume something is happening even though the audience can see that it isn't.

   – Please! Put that vase down!

Although the other actor may not have been holding a vase (or even thinking about holding a vase), on hearing the offer of endowment, they can accept it. Suddenly the vase appears, held aloft.

If this seems strange, consider theatre in Shakespeare's day. Elizabethan actors didn't always know every detail of the play they were performing, especially at the first performance. We know these plays weren't rehearsed as plays are now, if rehearsed at all, and the actors didn't possess the whole script, having instead only their lines and three words preceding their lines as a cue. So when Banquo says 'Look how our partner's rapt' (*Macbeth*, Act One, Scene Three), it serves as a prompt for the actor playing Macbeth. If he wasn't deep in thought, he had better become so now. Banquo *assumes endowment*. Macbeth accepts.

It's a different approach to the organic scene-building we were exploring earlier, but remember that there are a thousand ways to improvise and the tools in the toolkit are diverse.

Three-way Endowment

Play a short scene with two players.

Give the players a relationship and a location for the scene (so that they are not focusing on how to create it). For example:

- Two sisters playing volleyball.

- A mother and son standing in line for the cinema.

- A woman and her neighbour, in the driveway in front of their houses, about to take their children to school.

Ask player B to leave the room.

Player A must endow player B with a *characteristic*, e.g. overbearing, adorable, stinky… In this instance, let's say stinky.

Player A and the onlookers know the characteristic to be endowed. Only player B is unaware of their characteristic.

Bring back player B and ask player A to leave the room.

Now B learns how they must endow A, e.g. being drunk, fascinating, hilarious, or whatever. Let's say fascinating.

Have A and B improvise a scene for about three minutes, where they assume endowment of the other person. The endowment determines behaviour and behaviour drives the scene. In the above example, B will be fascinated by A, probably drawing close to them, whereas A will be repelled by B's smell, trying to get away. This simple dynamic provides plenty of opportunity for interaction.

When the scene is over, ask each player to guess their characteristic. If they guess correctly it is because the other player had endowed them clearly and effectively.

This exercise works very well with three players – A, B and C – each being endowed by the other two ('Stinky, Sexy, Funny' is a popular Keith Johnstone game).

Good endowments for this game include:

Sexy, funny, stinky, fascinating, childish, patronising, dangerous, drunk, stubborn, adorable, regal, catty, lazy, charming, impressive.

Tip: When playing with three players, try to avoid too many negative endowments. A scene with 'rude, angry and nasty' lacks contrast, whereas 'adorable, sexy and patronising' creates a better dynamic for interaction.

What happens if I missed an endowment?

It's improvised. We miss things sometimes. It happens. If you miss an endowment then you are involved in a new game – a game in which everyone knows what is going on except you! Listen to the audience responses and enjoy the game, no matter what context it takes. There are, in fact, numerous games dependent on players being unaware of their own endowment.

Chain Murder Endowment

This is an exercise for six players, though it can work with a few more.

All players, except one, leave the room. The solo player is given three pieces of information:

- A profession (e.g. a health-and-safety inspector).

- A room in a house (e.g. a wine cellar).

- A murder weapon (e.g. a draught excluder).

The more you play, the more detailed (or obscure) the specifics can become.

A team has five minutes to play the whole game.

It is played in gibberish (an invented nonsense language) throughout.

Player B enters and player A must attempt to communicate the profession, room and weapon to the new player. When the new player thinks they have all three answers, they murder the first player with the weapon.

The third player enters and the second player must now communicate the same information to them, until they too are murdered by the visitor.

And so on until all players have had their turn.

Then, starting with the last player and working backwards to the first, ask them what they think the profession, room and weapon were.

Things to look out for

Communication is a two-way process. It's not about one person frantically miming while the other person watches, waiting patiently or politely. The person receiving the information must make counteroffers so that both players can establish and agree on one offer before moving on to the next. If player A is trying to communicate 'gardening' to player B and player B thinks the profession is a gravedigger, they have to suggest it back to A.

> B (*miming a grave and someone dead inside it*). You mean like a gravedigger?

A can then correct them with an effective use of 'no':

> A (*miming pruning and watering plants*). No no. Nothing to do with death. A *gardener*.

Except all in gibberish, of course.

Keep up the time pressure of the game. It's more enjoyable played frantically against the clock.

Don't worry if it 'goes wrong' and you look foolish. Getting this game right is no fun at all.

Endless Guests

One player hosts a party. New guests arrive every thirty seconds. Each guest should enter with a strong, contrasting, emotional offer, and the host should immediately agree and build on it in a short exchange, before the guest moves into the party and another new guest arrives. The challenge is for guests and host to discover a shared backstory immediately.

For example:

> *The* HOST *opens the door to see* GUEST 1 *standing awkwardly, looking sheepish.*

> *The* HOST *makes an immediate assumption based on their observation.*

HOST. Did you hit my car again?

GUEST 1 (*wincing*). I'm so, so sorry.

HOST. Well, you'll have to pay for it this time, Rachel.

GUEST 1. I will, I will, I promise. Can I still come in?

> *And so on until* GUEST 2 *turns up, looking excited and energised, bursting with enthusiasm.*

HOST. You made it!

> *They embrace, jumping up and down with excitement.*

GUEST 2. Aarrrrghhhh! Of course I did. I wouldn't miss my best friend's party!

HOST. I thought your flight was cancelled?

GUEST 2. It was, I came by train.

> *Etc.*

> GUEST 3 *enters, speaking on her phone, ignoring the* HOST *and walking straight past.*

HOST (*deadpan*). Vodka's in the kitchen, Mum.

> *Etc.*

People can arrive in pairs or groups. Players can enter into the party and then leave the stage to make another entrance as a different character later. It is effective practice for short exchanges, instant agreement, characterisation, and entering with an offer rather than entering 'in neutral'.

Reality Clash

Ben Benison and Roddy Maude-Roxby taught me this game. Player A begins a scene with a clear endowment of the space and environment (e.g. a hotel). After a while B begins a scene in a contrasting environment (e.g. a boating lake). Without letting go of their own realities, each player finds ways to merge their reality with the other player's so that both can coexist and make sense.

I fondly remember an early performance of *Showstopper!* in which a scene began with Lucy Trodd frying sausages and Oliver Senton hanging up X-ray photographs. The audience started laughing because they could see both performers had created their realities at the same time, leading to a collision. Lucy glanced over at Oliver and said: 'I do hate it when you bring your work home with you.' With one line of dialogue the two conflicting realities were brought together to create a scenario in which a doctor is working so hard that he studies X-rays in his kitchen at home.

No Such Thing as a Mistake

There's a Netflix programme called *Chef's Table*, documenting the work of leading chefs from around the world, the first episode of which features Italian chef Massimo Bottura. When one of Bottura's cooks drops a lemon tart during service, the elegant dessert splatters all over the plate. The offending chef is devastated, convinced he has failed the exacting standards of the three-Michelin-starred kitchen. But Bottura looks at the shape of the dessert, splashed across the plate, and decides that *all* lemon tarts should now be presented in this exact manner – a vibrant explosion of colour. He even renames the dish 'Oops, I Dropped the Lemon Tart'.

There is no such thing as a mistake.

Jazz musician Miles Davis once said that no note on its own can be a mistake – it is the following note that defines and contextualises the previous one. It is one of the first things Dana Andersen told me when we started working together:

'You hit one bum note, it sounds wrong. Hit it a few more times and it sounds like a cool avant-garde tune.'

A mistake is a gift from the improv gods.

When improvising stories we not only work with mistakes, we make them critical to the narrative.

The novice student of improv is frightened of making mistakes, just as many of us are in life, and they often approach the subject as they would a subject at school. I have seen students wincing and stopping to apologise for things they think they have done wrong. Much of this comes from the legacy of our education systems, but much also derives from the heavy-handed, rules-based approach to improv favoured by many instructors today, where players are dogmatically told they *must do this* or they *must not do that. Don't ask questions. Where's the endowment? Stop being in your head!*

So can you make a mistake in improvisation? Well, who's to say what constitutes a mistake, other than the players while playing? As composer John Cage once put it: 'A mistake is beside the point, for once anything happens, *it authentically is.*'[13]

Say you called your scene partner Fran, then forgot that you had done so and accidentally renamed them Sally. Okay, you have a choice:

1. Pretend it didn't happen and carry on.

2. Work with someone who has two names.

3. Discover a reason why you confused the names.

The audience sees everything. Never pretend something hasn't happened. Everything authentically *is*. Accept the gift from the improv gods, explore the confusion, and the audience will delight in the liveness and danger of it all.

---

13. Jean-Jacques Nattiez (ed.), Robert Samuels (trans.), *The Boulez-Cage Correspondence*, Cambridge University Press, 1995, p. 107.

The moment an improviser thinks they have made some kind of 'mistake', they are apologising to the audience. Instead, working *with* these so-called mistakes is an essential part of the craft. There are no mistakes. How can there be? Nothing exists until the performers make something explicit.

For a *Showstopper!* performance in Brussels, the story was set at an international singing competition. We were approaching the interval, in the last few minutes of the first half, when there was a sound malfunction and a loud crack rang out. Everything stopped for a moment. Everyone in the audience had clearly heard it, and it sounded very out of keeping with everything else – in short, it sounded like a mistake. After a beat, the protagonist clutched his chest as if he had been shot and fell to the ground, dead. We were prepared to kill off our leading character by giving significance and meaning to apparent mistakes. The audience delighted in how spontaneous and daring the moment was. They also experienced a startlingly unexpected plot twist and a great cliffhanger. If our leading character was dead – what now? (Act Two took place in the afterlife, as I recall.)

Investing in the Environment

Where is this scene taking place?

Whether you have asked the audience to suggest this information or you are discovering it for yourselves, the setting fulfils several functions. It allows the players to find agreement on their playing space, how to stage themselves within it, and what the tone of their movement will be. People tend to move more slowly in a cathedral, for instance, and their behaviour changes accordingly.

The setting allows the audience to add their imagination to what they are seeing. Once the space has been endowed, audiences can't help but fill in the blanks.

The space can be symbolic, metaphorical or allegorical. It can represent, or stand in ironic contrast to, the characters and their stories. For example, a couple discussing the need for trust and security in their relationship while on a mountaineering wall, or installing a house alarm/CCTV system.

Be specific about where we are. Okay, it's a café, fine. Let's enjoy the details. Why is this scene set in this particular café? If you were writing the scene, why would you set it here? 'This is where we had our first date' gives the place meaning and significance. The characters could propose marriage to each other here or sign their divorce papers here – either way, it has meaning. We are investing in the environment.

You can invest in a scene *physically*.

Scenes that involve some aspect of engaging with the space are more enjoyable to watch and to play.

- This elevator is really crowded.

- Look at the space in this stretch limo!

- Come downstairs! I'm in the wine cellar.

- A secret door! Let's see where it leads.

You can use the space around you to invest in a scene *emotionally* ('My boyfriend dumped me in this diner').

Items, objects and furnishings are part of your environment. Invest in them, just as you do when dealing with the specifics of a scene. Doing so keeps everything related, increases our emotional investment in you, and deepens both character and dramatic action.

- My God. I remember this kite. Mum made it for me before she went to Alaska.

- This is the sword you used to kill my brother. Now I shall use it on you.

- Look, every couple in the village has scratched their initials on this tree.

- This is the *HMS Invincible*. My father was captain of this ship before me, and his father before him. This ship has been in my family's command for seven generations.

- There's an inscription inside this book: 'To H, thanks for the trip.'

Give your items and settings specific emotional significances, resonances, memories and meanings.

Discovering Through Environment

Imagine the audience has given you 'a bakery' as the setting for a scene.

Allow yourself to be suggestible on the idea of a bakery. Specifically, what kind of world is it? What kind of people might be found there? What is in the *circle of expectation* or related ideas? Ovens, early mornings, the smell of bread, flour, aprons, hygiene, sugar, cupcakes... whatever occurs to you.

- Two workers are decorating cupcakes in a trendy boutique bakery. The way they decorate their cakes suggests much about their personalities and characteristics. Roberta is precise and takes her time, Ravi is reckless and always seems to get away with it (maybe because Roberta always helps him out at the last minute).

Or:

- In a Detroit garage, Mitch has been struggling to fix up a car for months. This turns out to be symbolic of Mitch's recent estrangement from his brother.

In both these examples, the actors committed to ideas suggested by the environment, which were subsequently explored and fully integrated into the narrative.

Consider the watch prized by Butch (Bruce Willis) in *Pulp Fiction* – and the epic saga behind how it eventually reached Butch as a young boy; the clutched jacket in *Brokeback Mountain*; or the legacy of The Overlook Hotel in *The Shining*.

Specificity

Do you remember creative writing exercises at school? Sometimes the teacher would say: 'Write a story.' 'Well, what kind of story?' 'Anything you like,' was the reply. I remember finding it hard to know what to write, to know how to start. The blank page, with its infinite possibilities, was paralysing. But when the teacher provided a few sample titles, the imagination was quickly triggered.

Specificity is helpful for a number of reasons:

1. It gives the audience confidence in the performer.

2. It creates clarity.

3. It provokes connection and reaction.

4. It allows both audience and performer to find meaning in detail.

The novice improviser often finds specificity tricky. Like the pupil confronted with the blank piece of paper and the instruction: 'Write a story', insecurity prevents the player from making bold, clear, specific offers. So we get scenes like this:

A. So how's it going?

B. Yeah. Okay. It's alright.

A. Have you seen... you know?

B. Hmm, not sure.

A. Well, thanks for coming to meet me here. Outside.

B. No problem. It's okay.

A. I wanted to talk about the work you've been doing.

B. Oh yes. It is okay?

A. Yeah it's okay.

B. Yeah?

A. Well, you know.

This isn't ambiguous, it's vague. And the vagueness is strangling the scene. We don't know who these people are or where they are and, in this instance, not knowing isn't mysterious or in any way interesting. We get a 'feel', of course – something about working together, one calling the other to a meeting suggests a difference in status – but the scene isn't moving forward owing to a lack of specificity and a lack of commitment. The players are half-heartedly trying to endow each other, but nothing has any emotional weight. Everything is in the world of 'It's okay' – a safe place for anxious improvisers to occupy. Also note that the longer the scene goes on without specifics, the harder it can become for either person to be specific.

Be specific. Right from the start. There is no such thing as a mistake. Whatever specifics you introduce into the scene will be worked with and, as a consequence, become important.

With *specifics* the scene transforms. Take the opening line:

A. So how's it going?

If, instead, A was to observe B and see that B is a little sullen, downcast perhaps, the opening offer might be:

A. No need to be so worried, James.

B. Yeah. Okay. It's alright.

Being 'alright' is a glib, non-committal and undynamic place to be. But with acceptance and a stronger emotional stance:

B. I'm worrying. I can't help it. I'm a worrier.

A. Have you seen... you know?

Could be:

A. Have you seen Kathy from HR?

B. Hmm, not sure.

Could be:

B. Yes. She's looking for us and she's furious.

Now we have a situation, possibly a whole story. All the offers connect and we begin to discover who these people are, where they are and what their immediate situation is.

A character in a scene picks up a guitar. But what could that guitar be? You could endow the guitar in many ways:

- It's a 1968 Fender. My father used to play this when he was in a band.

- I was so jealous when Mum bought you this guitar.

- Do you remember when Mrs Adeyemi used to play this guitar around the campfire?

- I love this guitar. It's battered, missing a string, the fretboard is bust, but it reminds me of when I was on the road.

- I bought this guitar in Paris. The day I proposed to my fiancée.

- This is actually your guitar. I stole it from you two years ago.

- I haven't touched this guitar since Dad died.
- The Devil gave me this guitar.

Or, without dialogue, pick up the guitar and start crying, or laughing. Have a strong emotional connection and response. You don't even need to know why at the moment you do it – you can *discover* why later in the scene.

Specifics can generate meaning, emotion and character within seconds.

But how do I know what to say?

Allow yourself to be suggestible.

How do I know which specific to pick?

Go from your impulse driven by your observation of the other character(s).

It's like fishing in a stream with thousands of fish. If you try to catch 'the right fish' you will experience hesitancy and indecision. With practice, you simply cast the line and go with the first fish you catch.

Specificity should also be brought to your physicality, your engagement with the environment, how you mime objects or handle real props, and how you enter and exit the stage.

Guided Visualisation

I might use this exercise in a class with a student who is struggling to employ specifics. This could be out of fear, anxiety, a need to 'get it right', a desire 'not to screw up' or a fear of being judged for their contribution.

I make sure we are working in a quiet space without background noise. I ask the student to sit in a chair comfortably and close their eyes as I guide them through some visualisations. The rest of the group observe.

Sometimes I will simply ask: 'What can you see around you?' But if the student needs a little more time to relax and settle, I may have them step through an imaginary doorway or magic portal, some kind of threshold that they visualise. If they are still not forthcoming or claim not to be able to see anything, then I may start feeding them specific images: 'You are in a woodland. It's sunlit and warm. The trees are very green and very tall. Can you see them?'

Once the student is engaging and describing what they see around them, you can gently encourage them to be more specific.

A. I'm standing on a jetty.

B. Can you see any boats?

A. Yes.

B. Tell me about the one nearest to you.

A. It's like an old galleon, a pirate ship. Wooden, with big red sails.

B. Tell me about the figurehead.

A. It's a mermaid. With golden hair.

B. Can you read out the name of the ship written on the side?

A. Yes, *The Intrepid*.

You will be amazed at the level of detail these exercises can facilitate. When people are relaxed and engaged, you can have them go into imaginary libraries, pick up imaginary books and read out loud from them with startling fluidity. The students will surprise themselves.

Three Unrelated Things/Five Unrelated Things

This is an exercise for two players.

Player B suggests to player A three unrelated things – a person, a place and an object. These unrelated things must be specifically detailed. For example, B could say 'a salesman', but better to be more specific:

- *Person*: A sad second-hand-car salesman.

- *Object*: A shiny new toothbrush.

- *Place*: The back room of a convenience store.

Note that it's not just a car salesman, but a *sad* one, and a *second-hand dealer* at that. Not just a toothbrush, but one that positively *shines*. These details are not incidental – they must form the crux of a story so that it would be impossible to tell it about anyone or anything else. The emotional content and specificity is important.

There is no need for the storyteller to plan ahead or try to figure out where the story might go. They can simply start by putting any two elements together, exploring their meaning and relationship, and allow the story to emerge.

— There was once a sad second-hand-car salesman.

Prompt greater specificity in order to uncover story: 'Why sad?' Relate back to what you already have – reincorporate.

— He was sad because he didn't sell many cars and wasn't making a living. He dreamed of a showroom of gleaming new cars while trundling through life on a dwindling pocket. One day, he found in his bathroom cabinet a shiny new toothbrush. He didn't remember buying one, or being given one as a gift.

The storyteller has matched the salesman to the toothbrush. They still don't need to know exactly how the story will develop, but they continue to explore specifics, building on what they have already established.

Why is the shininess important?

— But he took out the shiny new brush and brushed his teeth with it. And his teeth began to shine. He kept using that toothbrush but it never lost its shine. Nor did his teeth.

Keep relating the ideas to each other.

— His smile began to look so dazzling that people
were drawn to him like never before. He started to
sell cars again.

By putting two elements together and exploring their emotional
significance, and by constantly reincorporating the key
elements, we can uncover the premise of our story. In this case,
what will happen to the car salesman now his fortunes have
turned around? And we will have other questions to explore:
Where did the toothbrush come from? We want to know what
happens next.

There are still specifics to work with here. Why are second-hand
cars essential to the story? Why not just 'a car salesman'? And we
should stick closer to a *shiny* toothbrush rather than a generically
magical one.

Exploring further by reincorporating, we could investigate the
idea of *shiny*.

— The more those old second-hand cars were
rusting, the shinier the salesman's smile became.
And he sold them all.

Work through the whole story in the same way.

Once players are comfortable with three unrelated things, they
can play with five:

• *Person*: A sad second-hand-car salesman.

• *Object*: A shiny new toothbrush.

• *Place*: The back room of a convenience store.

• *Object*: A Victorian hot-air balloon.

• *Object*: A battered, old flute case.

When coaching, keep reminding the storyteller to use specifics.
Why specifically a battered, old flute case? Why battered? Why a
flute? And why the case and not the flute?

Often you will observe the storyteller step back from the process
and try to put things into a context:

- Picture the scene. India. 1886. The sun hangs low in the sky. A cobra winds its way around a temple pillar...

This seldom works. The storyteller is moving further away from what the exercise demands of them and, when they do eventually engage with the key elements, it inevitably feels more contrived.

Just slam two of the 'unrelated things' together and explore from there.

It's a challenging exercise because players must remain committed and connected while moving through the unknown, with the growing realisation that they are approaching the ending of the tale without knowing how it ends.

Take your time with the exercise but resist the urge to race ahead and create context. Instead, keep looking backwards, refer to what you already have, and *recycle*.

'More Specific!'

Play a scene and coach the players with: 'More specific!' Explore the detail of whatever was just offered.

- I know where we can go for dinner.

'More specific!'

- I know this great place on Raynor Street, just up by the church.
- It's Greek–Swedish fusion.
- I hear the chef was involved in a car accident a few years ago and made this miraculous recovery.
- We went there once as kids. You were only five.
- They smash the plates at the end of the meal. You cried.

I have seen this played as a shortform performance game, with the audience shouting out 'More specific!' at any moment to compel an improviser to provide depth and detail.

Not every offer need be described in the same level of detail, otherwise a very dull scene might ensue, but bold, specific details are often required to keep a scene connected and moving forward.

If you want to climb a mountain, you're going to need to anchor a few pegs and find some secure footholds. Mountaineering is not for the vague.

Encourage players to be specific and to enjoy details rather than fear them, and to make emotional connections. A single, specific offer can contain enough emotional content for a whole story. Remember the character who hasn't touched the guitar since their father died? There's enough material to sustain an entire narrative right there.

Every idea has its opposite, and as much as specificity is helpful, there will be times when you may deliberately wish to avoid it.

The MacGuffin, a term popularised by Alfred Hitchcock, is something of great significance in a story that drives the plot but doesn't require specific detail.

We never know for sure what's in the suitcase in *Pulp Fiction*. We know that it glows with a golden hue and we see how people react to it, giving us a feel for how important it must be. Although people are prepared to kill for it, we never need to know what 'it' is.

Also consider:

- 'Rosebud' in Orson Welles' *Citizen Kane*.
- 'The Process' in David Mamet's *The Spanish Prisoner*.
- 'The One Ring' in *Lord of the Rings*.

What these mean to the characters in the stories is more important than the specific details of their function.

Activity

Activity, often referred to as 'business', is a physical task of some kind. Changing sheets on a bed, putting up a tent, going through tax returns, putting wedding invitations into envelopes, making a clay vase, repairing a car, etc.

Committing to an activity helps create a stage picture and adds specificity to the scene.

Undiscussed Activity

Play a scene with some kind of activity going on, but at no point do the players ever refer to it in any way. For example:

- Three office workers stuffing envelopes.

- Two criminals cracking a safe.

- A group preparing a meal in a kitchen.

The novice will often feel a need to refer to the activity, on occasion openly discussing how awkward the activity is making them feel, or how they don't want to do it. Embracing this game frees up the players from many negative tendencies and creates space for *relationships*.

Scenes with Symbolic Activity

Play scenes in which the activity becomes somehow symbolic of the action or feelings of the characters. For example:

- A couple playing chess while having a cagey discussion about fidelity.

- Two old rivals at a shooting gallery playing a status game with each other.

- Friends on a night out order cocktails with names that symbolise their mood or character – 'Make mine a Lucky Lady and I'll get a Shy Lotus for my quiet friend in the corner.'

Meaningful Activity

Investing in activities so they have meaning to the characters (and reincorporating those activities) can be rewarding. A play that ends as it begins, with two characters going through old photos in an attic, has a satisfying sense of completion to it. Reincorporating the activity gives it significance. Characters might build a house throughout the entire arc of a scene or story, as a metaphor for how they are coming closer together as friends.

Arranging one's books in alphabetical order might suggest a fastidious character, or serve as ironic contrast to the character's otherwise chaotic behaviour.

'You Look...' with Activity

'You Look...' exercises require people to face each other in a fairly neutral position, but you won't want many scenes to start that way. Have players begin a scene with activity, and as they observe each other, they can begin the 'You look...' organic scene-build as they continue.

For example, two players begin putting up a tent. Player A notices that player B is doing so with great joy. The *'You Look...'* game might lead them to something like this:

A. You look happy.

B. I am happy.

A. When I called, it sounded like you really needed to get away.

B. He's driving me mad. Couldn't wait to get out of the house. (*Looks around.*) There's a peg missing.

Here the missing peg could mean something is missing from the characters' lives, or it could be symbolic of something close to completion but frustratingly falling short. Maybe they find the peg quickly and move on. Maybe they don't find the peg until the final scene. Whatever happens gives both performer and audience information about the characters and their situation.

Joining and Contrasting

If I match you in tone, characteristics or activity, then I am *joining*.

If a scene begins with you anxiously digging and I join you, digging with the same anxiety, we suddenly appear to have history and connection. Even though, as performers, we may have no idea why we are digging, we *commit* to the activity, to the emotion, and build the scene together to discover what's going on.

When two, three or more performers all start joining at the top of a scene, it can be delightful to watch. The audience is fully aware that the players do not yet know the overall context of the scene.

I could also take a *contrasting* position. I could join you in digging (the activity), but I could contrast in mood (you are anxious, I am happy). Or I could contrast to you completely. I enter, don't dig, fiddle with my phone and watch, chuckling to myself. Now it's the *contrast* that provides the key starting elements to our scene. There are clear differences in status and emotion between us. Who are these people? What is their dynamic? Why is one character digging and the other just watching? Why is the digger anxious and the watcher laughing?

Quartets

Here's a more advanced game, but one that flexes lots of improv and scene-building muscles.

The scene begins with player A alone on stage. Give them an activity and an emotion, for example:

- Painting sadly.

- Cutting their own hair angrily.

- Putting up shelves wistfully.

Let the first part of the scene establish itself before player B enters. Allow player A to build the scene by developing the activity and deepening the emotion. Imagine it's like a game of *'What Happens Next?'* Keep working with the elements you are given – the activity and the emotion.

As a cue to enter, player B is waiting for some kind of beat change, a rhythmic interruption, or the completion of a unit of action – often ways in which you would design the scene if it were scripted.

Player B enters, and both players now establish a platform so that we know who they are, what their relationship is, and where the scene takes place. We will also discover the 'what' of the scene, i.e. the basic premise, informed no doubt by the emotion of player A and the reactions of player B.

When player C joins the scene, the players' job is to raise the stakes/to put heat under what is already there/to intensify meaning or emotional significance.

Finally, when player D enters, the players have one minute in which to finish the scene.

Things to look out for

These tasks don't solely fall to the new player entering the scene. It is always a collective responsibility. For example, player C enters the scene and after a while it might be player A or B, affected by something player C has done, who raises the emotional stakes. Or player D might come on stage without a single idea of how to conclude the scene, but between them all four players, using reincorporation, will find an ending.

Very often player D will carry out the same function as player C, trying to create a new drama rather than making an offer to unify the group in agreement. Or the players will start arguing, forgetting there is only a minute left in which to conclude the scene. This game is a good training to help players understand when to be in conflict and when to look for harmony.

Sometimes the ideas are obvious and come easily. Other times players will freeze, refusing to enter the scene, because they don't have an idea in their heads and don't know what to contribute. Encourage them to jump in anyway and keep things moving forward by using observation and connection. Something will emerge. Remind the players that nothing will progress if they are all stuck offstage worrying about what to do. Step into the unknown!

Competence

Improvised scenes generally benefit from characters being competent at their activities. Bearing in mind the importance of a scene's forward movement, being capable enables some momentum.

The inexperienced improviser tends towards playing incompetent characters ('Surgery? Oh, I don't know how to do that' or 'Surgery? Well, yes but it's my first day'). This is a protective measure to minimise risk. We are less likely to be judged for failing at something after declaring we don't know how to do it. Such scenes rarely have forward movement, and the audience becomes aware that the performer is, in fact, revealing their own incompetence or insecurity.

Playing a competent, skilled and capable character gives you, your fellow players and the audience, confidence. It allows you to progress so that you can discover what is important in the scene.

There are ways to play incompetent characters, but it is advisable for students to develop competence as a habit first.

Superheroes

Play a scene in which players endow each other as superheroes with superpowers.

Try all sorts – silly ones, inspiring ones, or powers that genuinely crop up within the genre. Battle against a world-threatening crisis or deal with a mundane everyday situation, it doesn't matter. Playing superheroes or anyone with superpowers will push players to embrace competence.

Shopping Channel (page 33)

Sales patter requires commitment and competence.

Arms Through

A very popular old improv game in which one player stands with their arms behind their back and a second player stands behind the first, feeding their arms through in order to play the first person's arms. The first player delivers a lecture on a subject given to them by the audience.

Remember: communication is a two-way process. As the speaker makes emotional changes the arms must follow – but the arms can also make offers that the speaker must follow too.

It's fun to play with a number of arms-through characters at the same time, all meeting at a party or event.

Translated Lecture

A similar game with two players in which one speaks in a gibberish language (on a subject given by the audience) while the second player translates a phrase at a time. Make sure the lecture has emotional change and development, so as to avoid the same undynamic delivery experienced initially in the word-at-a-time-story games.

Three-headed Expert

A recurring game for the Comedy Store Players. A single expert with three heads speaks about (or is interviewed on) a topic suggested by the audience. The three performers playing the expert speak one word at a time.

Dubbing

This game can be played with any number of people but usually is best started with two players on stage and two onlookers at the front of the audience, facing the action.

The onstage players have their dialogue voiced by the two onlookers. As with translation games or *Arms Through*, players may need to be reminded it is a two-way process. If the onstage character starts moving their mouth, the dubber had better put some voice to it immediately, and if the dubber starts voicing, the onstage actor must start owning the content. Once more, responsibility is shared among the group, as the game's restraints mean no single person can control the action too much.

When these sorts of games are played for the first time, all scene-building skills tend to go out the window, and you may observe players arguing, much as they did at the start of their training. Encourage performers to play a scene as they normally would, with endowment, forward movement, emotional change and reincorporation.

Emotional Change/Development

In preparation for our first attempt at a thirty-six-hour improvised soap opera, director Dana Andersen suggested the following way of playing a scene:

1. Build a platform – who are you, where are you, and what's going on?

2. Emotional change – something changes emotionally for one or more characters.

3. Reincorporate to finish – bring back an idea, motif or detail from earlier.

Look at scripted scenes for stage or screen. They often have some kind of platform and development before we find out *what the scene is really about.*

It's a useful question, asked frequently by fellow teacher and Showstopper Dylan Emery, and one I often ask in the rehearsal room when I am watching scenes:

'What's this scene *really* about?'

As the old screenwriters' maxim has it: *If the scene is about what it's about then you're in trouble.* A scene may have two work colleagues talking about what kind of coffee they prefer, but what's the subtext? What is the relationship between them? What is at stake? What is the coffee discussion masking? *What is the scene really about?*

What matters to these characters? If nothing matters to them, then after a while it won't matter to us either. Emotional development is essential in a story – in any kind of narrative and longform improv – and often extremely beneficial to shortform scenes. Cut the glib stuff and allow characters to be affected by each other.

Dana taught the following game to practise this:

'You F**king Liar'

Have two players begin a scene.

Give them some information to start with or let them discover it themselves, but let them build a platform, either using a three-line initiation, an organic scene-build, or any other approach. Let them establish who they are, where they are, and what the dynamic is between them.

Any time after the platform is built, one player says to the other: 'You F**king liar!' (Replace expletive as desired.)

The player accused of being a liar must now go through three different emotional reactions *before anyone can say anything more in the scene.*

Don't rush it. Make sure time is taken to go through three clearly different emotional responses. And make sure those emotional changes are critical to the development of the scene. For example:

A and B are sisters. B is about to sing on a TV talent show. They are backstage.

- A. No one supports you more than me.

- B. You f**king liar!

    A is shocked and reeling for a few moments, then she starts to laugh, and eventually becomes sad, putting her head in her hands.

- A. You're right. I'm selfish. I wish I was the one up there.

A and B are both changed and affected by the emotional development of the scene, which cannot go back to how it was before the accusation was made.

Overaccepts

This is based on a game by Keith Johnstone.

Set up a scene. Keep it simple to begin with and limit it to two or three players.

At any point in the scene, on the bell, one player must *overaccept* whatever has just been offered. It can be verbal or non-verbal, but it has to be a huge emotional reaction to the previous beat.

- (*Outraged.*) Do I want toast? You talk about toast at a time like this? How could you?

- (*Crying.*) Toast? It reminds me of when I used to live in Lakeview. I loved that house. I miss those days.

– (*Ecstatic.*) Toast! I love toast! I – Are you serious?
I would absolutely love a piece of toast right now.
You really are the most thoughtful and generous
person I know.

I have watched Die-Nasty's Jeff Haslam energise (and save) many
a scene by overaccepting and by being utterly fascinated in his
scene partner.

Putting heat under what's there

Novice improvisers often turn their backs on what is
happening in a scene and start broadening into numerous
disconnected ideas, which can be difficult for their colleagues
to work with, let alone watch. The pressure to come up with
something interesting, and the speed with which a player can
lose interest in a situation because they do not know where it
might lead, causes disconnection from their partners and the
scene-building alike.

If something crops up in a scene and you feel an impulse from
it – *put some heat under it*. Explore it. Further it. Make it
matter more. Intensify it.

Emotional Taxi

One of my favourite games (and a big favourite with students at
LAMDA).

Set up some chairs to represent a taxi – two at the front and three
at the back, or however you want to make it work.

One player is designated the driver and the other four are
passengers. The group assigns each passenger an emotion
before the game begins and everyone knows each other's
emotions. Play with a mix of negative and positive, and aim for as
much contrast as possible. For example:

A = Joyful

B = Paranoid

C = Cheeky

D = Adoring

The taxi driver begins with a solo scene, building a platform and developing it on their own, until player A enters the taxi. Both actors switch to A's emotion – *joyful*. After a while, the driver picks up character B, who joins the first two, and they all switch emotion to become *paranoid*. When character C joins the group everyone becomes *cheeky*, and eventually all five players are in the taxi with their behaviour being driven by the emotion *adoring*.

The taxi driver can then drop off each passenger one by one, all switching back to the previous group emotion as they go, until only the driver is left to complete the scene alone. At the start and the end of the game, when the driver is alone, they may play any emotions they wish. Being affected by the various emotions experienced throughout their journey, and reincorporating details from the very start of the game, will make for more a satisfying narrative. I once saw a player begin the game as the driver, failing to get a fly out of his taxi with increasing desperation. By the time he had picked up and dropped off all his passengers, he had learned how to calmly open the window and let the fly out.

Scenes in Gibberish

Scenes in which players cannot use recognisable language and must speak in a made-up gibberish are excellent practice for improvisers. In order for these scenes to sustain they must have emotional content, drive and contrast, and players must find agreement, even in the abstract. Test your group by seeing how long they can sustain scenes in this way.

Play the variants on this game too, e.g. one speaking in gibberish, the other in English, and switching between the languages.

Songs in gibberish are fun and highly recommended if there is a musician in your group who can accompany you on piano or guitar, although a capella gibberish songs are also worth experimenting with.

Removing the wordy aspects of improv, where everything becomes primarily driven by what people say, and eliminating the tensions this can create, is often beneficial.

Reincorporation

As mentioned earlier, reincorporation is the bringing-back of things, the recalling of events and motifs that have happened earlier. Sometimes referred to as a 'callback', reincorporation is essential in effective storytelling. It's story cement that keeps everything together.

It's often easier for a performer to reincorporate an offer or idea rather than 'thinking something up' or creating anything new.

Some ideas are so powerful that, if they are *not* reincorporated, the audience rightly feels cheated. When they are reincorporated, especially towards the end of a scene or narrative when the audience has mostly forgotten (or suspect the players have forgotten), they can elicit squeals of delight.

Our *Showstoppers' Kids Show* is an interactive musical improv show for kids. We only take suggestions from the kids and their ideas are almost always hilarious, innovative and perfectly suited to wherever we are in the story. As we begin to reach the end of the narrative, the children intuitively know what needs to happen. They understand the concept of reincorporation even though they probably wouldn't know what to call it.

– The Mermaid Queen comes back.

– He remembers what his mother told him.

– She goes back home.

Kids, immersed in the world of story, can craft one very well. They certainly appreciate the importance of reincorporation.

In the last part of a scene or story we might not want to add much, if any, new information. This structure is often referred to as the *narrative diamond*. We begin with one point and one idea (the bottom point of the diamond) which broadens out to its widest point (the middle). Then the themes and ideas are recycled and revisited until the shape closes back up to a single point (the opposite tip of the diamond). Reincorporation moves us towards conclusion. Many stories end in the exact place they started. Tolkein's *The Hobbit* is subtitled *There and Back Again*.

One Player Can Only Reincorporate

This is based on a game by Keith Jonhnstone.

Play any kind of scene or game (preferably with a few players) in which one player cannot generate or create anything new, but can only reincorporate offers that have already been made by other players. They can use any words, activities, actions or emotions they see around them and may reincorporate as many times as they wish.

Musical Reincorporation

Sing 'The Twelve Days of Christmas' – it always comes back to where it started, with a partridge in a pear tree.

If you have musical improvisers in your group, make up other songs like this.

In fact, pretty much any form of musical improvisation, which requires a chorus or a hook that people can return to, is good practice for musical and non-musical improvisers alike.

Three Unrelated Things/Five Unrelated Things (page 109)

These games compel you to reincorporate in order to find the meaning and ending of stories.

Book Launch (page 34)

Book Launch encourages the performer to recycle themes and material from the pages as they read aloud, before the book is taken away. The more the player reincorporates, the easier and more successful the improvised continuation of the book becomes.

The Ideas Board

Italian troupe I Bugiardini sometimes improvise a story with someone sitting to one side of the stage, writing notes on a whiteboard as the action unfolds. These notes can include obvious details, such as the location or characters of the first scene, or smaller details, such as an object, a character trait, or simply something that has been said. At any time, an improviser in the story can raise their hand, at which point the whiteboard of ideas is revealed to them and they can use anything that has been written on it. Players can raise their hands when they feel stuck for ideas, demonstrating that any number of ideas can be reincorporated to move the scene forward, freeing improvisers from the pressure to be overinventive.

Ending Scenes Using Reincorporation

Bringing back almost anything from the start of your scene or game will create a sense of completion, of coming full circle.

Remember this scene from earlier?

A (*startled*). Professor Jenkins, it's gone midnight, what are you doing in the museum?

B (*suspicious*). Sarah. I might have known my most conscientious student would still be here.

A (*trying to be friendly*). Need some help with those fossil samples?

This scene begins in a museum after midnight with a professor and student in a cagey, suspicious dynamic. There are any number of ways it could develop, but reincorporation of the time (gone midnight), the activity (fossil samples) or anything else already known to the audience will naturally lead us towards a sense of conclusion.

B. So now you know the whole story. Help me get these fossil samples out of here before we're both caught.

Or:

A. I'm sorry, professor, I really am. I wish things could have been different. But right now I'm taking these fossil samples with me. And if you know what's good for you, you'll never breathe a word of this to anyone.

Or how about this scene from earlier:

A. You look excited.

B. I am excited, Jack.

A. Me too. Everyone's coming tonight.

B. Really? Everyone's coming to my little leaving party?

A. This office won't be the same without you, Katie.

B (*excited*). Is Steve coming?

A. I guess so. (*Moves away, a little hurt.*) He is our boss after all.

Any of these opening elements can be reincorporated – the party, Steve, Jack's unrequited attraction to Katie, leaving the office or a physical detail of the playing space. Which of the many options you pick in the moment will depend on what you feel the scene is primarily about. If you feel the scene is about Jack's unrequited attraction, then you will probably reincorporate something in this sphere. If you feel Katie's excitement about Steve is most important, reincorporate those elements.

Don't know what to do? Try reincorporating something without knowing why. Remember: you do not have responsibility for the whole scene. It is shared. Others will work with you.

Action

In the study of acting, an *action* is a single moment in which one actor attempts to affect the other. It is a tactic employed in the moment in the pursuit of an intention. The action is denoted with a transitive verb, for example:

- I placate you.
- I tease you.
- I condemn you.
- I repel you.
- I embrace you.
- I impress you.
- I beg you.

(Etc. – There are thousands of transitive verbs.)

Playing Actions

Ask one actor to select their favourite line of dialogue from a play or film. It can be anything from 'If music be the food of love, play on' to 'Hasta la vista, baby!' Have them deliver their line to every other person in the room, one at a time, giving them a different action to play with each new target:

- I enthrall you.
- I attack you.

- I educate you.

- I provoke you.

...and so on.

It is essential that the actor be outwardly focused. The performer is not attempting to feel or create any kind of emotional state for themselves, but is instead doing whatever is required to affect other people in the scene. In playing the action 'I seduce you', an actor might direct their focus inwardly, in order to feel and try to inhabit a general state of sexiness. This is likely to look strange and not at all seductive because it is unspecific, inwardly focused, and therefore has no relation to a target. The actor must look at their target. How would you seduce them in this moment? Might you want to make them smile, or simply get them to look at you, or hold their eye contact in a different way? The answer, as Meisner reminds us, 'is in the other guy'.

When I coach actors on text – working on a speech, for example – I often notice the actions change rather slowly: there isn't enough contrast between them. If the actors were to play *fast contrasting actions* – I hate you, I need you, I reject you, I embrace you (moving quickly from one extreme to the other) – their acting would have more volatility and danger. Observe any couple in a heated argument and you will see fast contrasting actions played out.

You don't need scripted lines to play fast contrasting actions. As an improviser you are playing beats and offers just as you would in any drama. Embrace change, try to affect the other person, and allow yourself to be affected by them.

Contrasting actions are also effective ways of showing confusion or awkwardness. Many actors adopt a sustained or generic state of confusion in order to 'appear confused', but this doesn't play well in performance. Confusion, as anyone who has ever watched Stan Laurel's eyebrows will tell you, is best shown with *contrast*, i.e. 'I've got it! Oh, no I haven't. Wait, yes I have! Oh, actually… hang on…'

Be careful not to compress multiple actions into a vague and sustained emotional state. One of the best notes I was ever given as an actor was that 'no single emotional state lasts longer than ten seconds'.

Status

Status is your position within a social hierarchy in relation to others.

This is often tricky to analyse because:

1. We exist in a number of different hierarchies/groups.

2. Status is relational and therefore often in flux.

3. Different people perceive us differently.

There are many contributing factors to status and they can be culturally specific – competence and charisma may carry more importance in some arenas than wealth and power.

There is also a difference between *status* and *rank*. David Brent (Ricky Gervais's character in *The Office*) ranks higher than his staff, being their boss, but his desperate need for popularity lowers his status. In *The King's Speech*, George VI holds the highest rank of all, but speaking in public with a pronounced stammer undermines his status. Fools in Shakespeare's plays are usually low in rank but can be granted high status when monarchs want to hear their wisdom.

We may experience a difference in status when moving from one social group to another – among groups of friends, family units and work environments, for example. Our status often fluctuates within a group. Or within even a single conversation. Observe almost any scenes from scripted drama and you will see the characters raise and lower their status many times. The rise and fall of Macbeth's status is the narrative arc of classical tragedy.

Most importantly, status is an interaction. As an essential part of human communication, it's worth devoting some time to in the study and practice of improvisation.

Status Greeting

To begin with I use a game taught to me by Ben Benison and Roddy Maude-Roxby. Two actors stand at opposing ends of the room. They walk past each other and greet each other in some way (vocally – they must make a sound). By the time they get to the other side, the rest of the group votes – who was the servant and who was the master? Sometimes it is startlingly clear, other times the distinctions are finer, but the students are learning to pick up *status behavioural indicators*.

It's worth emphasising that 'master' and 'servant' are not pejorative terms.

High-status behavioural indicators

- Ease of movement and speech.
- Open gestures.
- Doing things in their own time.
- Seemingly less affected by things.
- Unapologetic.

Low-status behavioural indicators

- Erratic, extraneous and unnecessary movement.
- Hesitant or interrupted speech patterns.
- Ill-at-ease.

- Diminished body space.

- Apologetic.

- Eager to please.

- Easily affected by things.

In improvisation, to endow another player as being higher status is simply a starting offer. Who knows how status will have changed by the end of the scene?

Much of clowning, indeed comedy in general, is based around status transactions. Clowns can even be lower status than their *environment* – the clown trying to put up the deckchair, for example. Peter Sellers' Inspector Clouseau is a high-ranking detective who believes himself to be high status, whilst clumsily losing status to objects and furniture around him.

Sometimes a low-status character can garner so much attention they become high status, such as an adorable baby in a room full of fawning adults. A person can strive for status so awkwardly that they become low status (MC Grindah from the BBC's *People Just Do Nothing*).

Abstract Instructions

Once players are paired as master and servant from the *Status Greeting* exercise, I have them play short (three-minute) scenes without dialogue, in which the master makes a series of abstract gestures that the servant interprets as commands before carrying them out. The game works on agreement – the master always accepts that whatever the actor playing the servant does is exactly what the master had intended, e.g. the master claps their hands and the servant pours them a drink, or the master holds up three fingers and the servant starts to dance for them. Any signal can be met with any response.

In these games, watch out for masters correcting their servants, for they lose status when they do so, and encourage servants to be playful and more daring with their interpretations. Keep a close eye on the staging of the interaction. Which moves and positions on the stage raise or lower status? (More on this later.) It's a game – players do not have to be literal in their interpretations of the commands. They are looking to have fun and provoke each other through clowning.

An understanding of status can drive an entire scene. Try the following examples, bringing back the option of dialogue:

- Character A is a low-status master and character B is A's high-status servant. Today A must cut B's pay.

- Character A is the master and B is the servant, but they are both low status. They must compete to be the lowest-status character throughout the scene.

- A and B as master/servant but both are high status.

- A is a high-status master and B is a low-status servant, but by the end of the scene A has become a low-status master and B has become a high-status servant.

Things to look out for

High status does not have to mean cruel. Low status does not have to mean stupid. There are myriad ways of exploring the extremes of status. Keep experimenting and observing *behavioural indicators*.

A shift in status can be enough dramatic interaction to sustain a whole scene (or, in the case of Harold Pinter's film *The Servant*, an entire story).

Fast Status Switch

Play a scene in which the status switches every six seconds, indicated by a bell. Alternatively, you may switch after every three lines/offers.

Notice that these status switches often induce laughter.

Status is especially important in three-character scenes. Try some with the following dynamic:

- A high-status to B, but low-status to C.
- B low-status to A, but high-status to C.
- C therefore is high-status to A and low-status to B.

Group Status Greetings

Players move around the room at a relaxed, natural walking pace. Ask them all to raise their status so they are competing to become the highest-status person in the group. People must still greet each other by vocalising something as they pass by. Repeat the exercise with low-status interaction.

You will probably observe the tempo in the room slowing down in the high-status competition, and speeding up when the group shifts to low status. Players will often refrain from speaking when high status, but must be reminded to do so as it's an important part of the transaction.

Ask the players if they experienced an interaction with someone who raised or lowered their status. What happened to make them feel that way? Was there one person who seemed genuinely higher or lower than everyone else throughout?

Play a scene in which two young children are higher status than their parents.

Play a solo scene in which the actor plays both the roles of master and servant, switching between the two. Note the cruelty that all masters suddenly seem to inflict upon their servants when both roles are played by the same performer.

Status Parties

Have ten players draw from ten playing cards, ace to ten. The ace is the lowest-status character in the group, the ten is the highest. Players only know their own status card. They then begin a short scene, at a party or a doctor's waiting room, or some such simple setting, and interact according to their status number. They must display *status behavioural indicators* to signal their value to the others.

It is worth reminding the players that they must find reasons to interact with every other member of the group throughout the exercise. If the group does so effectively, the rest of the class watching should be able to line up the players in correct order of status after approximately five minutes of observation.

You can play versions of this game without dialogue, emphasising that behaviour is often more important than words. Or you can vary the cards in the deck, so that you might have two aces in play without the players knowing, leading to some very interesting, and often entertaining, status clashes.

Secret Status Party

Play a variation where each player is given one card, placing it immediately on their forehead so that they cannot see its value but all their fellow players can. Set these improvisations at some kind of social gathering. As the group interacts, players endow each other with the status displayed on their foreheads.

I add an endowment to this game, ascribing each suit with a quality, alliterative for ease of remembering:

Clubs = cute

Diamonds = dangerous

Hearts = hilarious

Spades = sexy

Meeting someone with the king of spades (high-status, sexy) on their forehead would require an endowment of powerful and attractive, while someone with the two of hearts (low-status, hilarious) on show might be treated as if they were amusing but not to be taken seriously. The three of diamonds (low-status, dangerous) might suggest endowing someone as drunk, reckless and a little annoying.

Again, if the group endows status and quality effectively, after around ten minutes of interaction each player should be able to take a guess as to what value card they were given.

Patterns

Back at the start of our training we improvised a ballet in which any movement offered by a performer is repeated by other members of the group. This immediate agreement gives the ballet a sense of choreography and design. Patterns are created from observation and repetition.

I remember watching a show in which a messenger came in to deliver some news but tripped up by accident on the way to the stage. From that point on, every time any messenger entered they stumbled in the same way. Repetition of the so-called 'mistake' created a pattern or game.

Discovering and developing patterns gives each scene shape and structure.

I have found this little maxim to be very useful:

'If It's Good, Make It Better; If It's Bad, Make It Worse.'

Here 'good' and 'bad' can refer to events happening not only to the characters (are they having a good day or a bad day?), but also to the craft of improv itself.

For example, if a player who is hysterical and full of negativity crashes into a scene, it can unsettle others on stage. However, if everyone allows themselves to be affected by increasing their own hysteria and negativity, the scene will start to have a feeling of design about it. By recognising and developing a pattern, everyone will be playing the same game. Many improvisers are problem-solvers by nature and see it as their responsibility to negate or neutralise such offers, but sometimes it's best to go deeper into what is already there.

Hand of Misère

There is a scene in Steven Spielberg's film *Jaws* in which the three principal characters compare scars and injuries. It becomes a competition, each revealing a more dangerous encounter or story ('Well, I've got something worse than that...').

Conor McPherson's play *The Weir* is a series of ghost stories, each more disturbing than the last.

I know this game as *Hand of Misère*, often played with the set-up of some kind of 'survivors' group', each member of which shares a more harrowing story than the last. The game tests a group's ability to move forward in gradual increments. If the first speaker's offer is too wild, it can become challenging for subsequent players to develop the scene.

It should be noted that the nature of the game encourages escalation and transgression. While often played for comic effect, I have explored *Hand of Misère* with actors in training who have approached it very seriously. And why not? Improvisation might still be perceived as a comedic form, but with the right group and in certain contexts, compelling drama can also result.

The opposite conceit – 'make things better' – can also be explored.

Settings might include a group of youngsters in a summer camp sharing what good news they have received in letters from home, or a reunion of friends catching up with what they are up to now in their lives, with each boast more impressive than the last.

There is a scene in the film *Bridesmaids* in which two women publicly compete for the favour of their bride-to-be best friend, each speech and anecdote becoming increasingly emotional and personal.

The Game of the Scene

This is a phrase popular in US short- and longform improv, and one over which there is much confusion and disagreement. A number of definitions have been offered.

The game in question might be an articulation of an emerging pattern played by some or all of the group. Others define it as the first beat outside the pattern, the first 'curveball' or offer outside the circle of expectation. To some the game can be purely personal, something for the performer to amuse themselves with. I've also heard it articulated as 'something a player does that others would like to see them do more of'. It could be a characteristic that encourages comedy. Sitcoms do this all the time, where characters change less, if at all, and are driven instead by familiar characteristics. In *Fawlty Towers*, Basil Fawlty is uptight; in *Friends*, Monica is neurotic and Phoebe is dippy.

For me the *scene* is what's happening between the characters and the *game* is what's happening between the players. Improvisation thrives on the elements of game because the audience is aware of the players discovering everything in the moment. There is less desire to hide the mechanics of theatrical processes and create the verisimilitude favoured in most forms of theatre.

For example, if the scene is a job interview:

A game unintentionally unfolds when both actors realise they were inconsistent in their placement of an imaginary door on the set – a 'mistake'. But the rest of the players turn the 'mistake' into a game and keep dropping in and out of various 'doors' throughout the scene.

Remember: if it's good, make it better; if it's bad, make it worse.

Or, in the same setting:

A game emerges when one player notices they have used a lot of words beginning with the letter 'P'. Sensing it as an emerging pattern, they continue to use as many 'P'-words as possible. The second player, noticing this, embarks on a letter-'S' spree.

None of this impairs the scene, which is still a job interview, but the audience is aware that the actors are simultaneously discovering some kind of game – in this instance, a linguistic one.

There are thousands of ways to play games in scenes. Listen, observe, play with patterns, listen to your audience – either games will emerge and you will play them, or they won't. Don't stress over it.

Character

One of the most problematic questions in the subject of acting is: What is character?

Aristotle suggests character is habitual action. 'We are what we repeatedly do. Qualities of character emerge as a result of our actions.'

Robert McKee refines this somewhat, describing it as 'choice under pressure'. In the Paul Haggis film *Crash*, a number of characters appear as familiar types we know and understand, until they are placed in pressured situations in which the choices they make, and their resultant actions, reveal who they truly are.

Have you ever had a friend who is struggling in their relationship with their partner – a partner whose words are inconsistent with their actions?

Our character is determined by what we repeatedly do. We are the choices we make and the actions we take as a result, things that become more acutely revealed under pressure. The manner in which we carry out these actions may be described as *characteristics*.

In *True and False*, David Mamet suggests: 'There is no such thing as character.'[14] At first glance it may appear to be a

14. David Mamet, *True and False: Heresy and Common Sense for the Actor*, Faber and Faber, 1998, p. 9.

provocation (indeed, much of the book is a reaction to the 'Method' school of acting). But, contrary to much common thought on the subject, it can be empowering for an actor not to think about their character, and instead to trust that when they commit to their lines with *outward focus* and *intention*, a character *emerges*.

It may help to think that character is more *perceived* than it is *portrayed*.

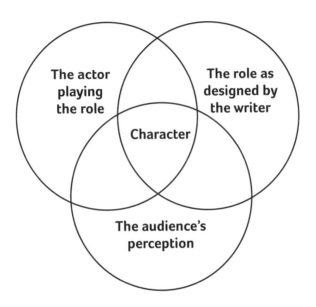

In improvisation, we cannot fully know what character we are playing until we reach the end of the story. How can we? Our actions and choices are made in the moment, and sometimes other performers endow our character with actions when we are not even on stage. Actors in a long-running television series, like a soap opera, also work this way. A script can arrive at any time, revealing that their character is involved in something wholly unexpected. A character has been undercover, or has been secretly embezzling, or has been having an affair. All are events that neither actor nor audience anticipated.

Del Close encouraged his players to 'wear their character thinly like a veil' to encourage the actors to begin scenes naturally, as themselves, allowing subtle changes and variations to emerge through the playing of the scene.

Once again, there is no single formula. You can make choices at the start, during the scene or before the scene even begins – it doesn't matter. What's more important is that, at any time, you are prepared to let go of what you think something *ought to be* in favour of responding to what *authentically is*, i.e. what is actually happening.

I remember an early *Showstopper!* show, set in the world of spies in 1940s Cairo. Throughout the story I had played the villain's wizened henchman, a comic character who didn't have much to do with the narrative. In the final scene, the villain was vanquished and said to the hero: 'My God, you're good!' To which the hero replied: 'Yes, I'm good…' And here the actor walked over to me and put his hand on my shoulder before continuing: 'But not as good as Special Agent Philip Smythe of the Special Operations Executive.'

I stood up to my full height for the first time and said, 'Thank you very much, sir,' in a clipped British accent.

I had been undercover this whole time. I didn't know this until now. But my character knew. Philip Smythe always knew.

'My character wouldn't do that'

How many of us can truly say we completely understand our own character, let alone someone else's?

As an actor, rehearsing a play, you are following instructions from a manual called The Script. The actor who says: 'My character wouldn't do that' is really saying: 'I don't want to do that' or 'I don't feel comfortable doing that.' In working with actors for many years I have observed that the lines causing them the most discomfort are vitally significant because these are the moments when the actor feels most different from the character they are playing. Embracing that difference can be revelatory.

In narrative improvisation you don't even have a character until the whole thing is over. I didn't know I was undercover agent Philip Smythe until the very end of the story. My character was a gift given to me by another player. Usually, if an improviser insists their character wouldn't act in a certain way, it's an indication of that performer's rigidity, of them resisting change and closing down avenues of exploration. The moment you feel yourself resisting offers from your group because you don't think they fit your character, remind yourself that you can never know all the details of your character until the final seconds of the performance. You are what you agree to. The choices you make under pressure will determine what sort of character you become.

In traditional text-based acting the actor is cast in a role, spends time getting familiar with that role, goes to rehearsals, discovers more about the mechanics and psychology of the play as a whole, makes choices, experiments, hones in advance of an opening night, adds costume, set, lights, sound and finally... *arrives* at the first performance. In improvisation, however, the actor begins with the opening night and a complete performance, working backwards, so that by the time they have finished the show they discover what the story was and what they had been playing.

In improv you cannot decide what kind of character you are going to play before a scene starts because your character will be revealed over time through a series of actions. You can only decide where to begin your journey. You can, however, make choices about your *characteristics*.

Jill Bernard's delightful *Small Cute Book of Improv* offers an acronym for instant characteristics. 'VAPAPO' stands for:

- *Voice* – Use a different accent or register of your voice.
- *Attitude (or Emotion)* – Start a scene with a strong emotional choice.
- *Posture/Physicality* – Change to a higher- or lower-status physical position. Move at a different tempo.
- *Animal* – Let any animal inspire your mood and movement.
- *Prop* – Use a real or mimed prop, such as a walking stick or basketball.
- *Obsession* – Fixate on something so that it has real importance to you.

Jump into a scene having made a strong choice on any of the above and you will appear and behave differently.

Rhythm and Tempo

Scenes and characters have their own tempos and rhythms. A churchyard at night immediately implies a slow pace punctuated with small, sudden spooks. The floor of the London Stock Exchange suggests fast-tempo, staccato rhythms and high pressure. Allow the setting to be an offer that affects you. Just as you receive impulses by making eye contact with someone, you also receive them from changing your speed and physicality. *Contrasting* your character's tempo with your environment can be interesting too – picture one child moving slowly and methodically in a bouncy castle while other kids around her are leaping in all directions.

Do you have a default tempo as a performer? Are you always fast and frenetic, or measured and careful? Do you play all situations and settings the same way? Try exploring variety.

Character Switch

Performers A and B play a scene. On the bell, performer A switches to become character B, and B in turn plays character A. Players should be encouraged to switch physical positions and become the other character with as much accuracy as possible. How was the other character standing? What tempo, energy, rhythm or other defining characteristic needs to be observed and replicated? What were they in the middle of saying or doing that needs to be continued? The performers carry on with the same scene, now playing the other character.

Allow a little time to establish the scenario and characters before you ring the bell, then escalate the rate of switching as the game goes on. Players will have to make sure that their characters are contrasting. This is not a time for joining. You will soon see who is paying attention to their scene partner and who is too preoccupied with themselves to be outwardly focused and receptive.

Point of View

Some schools of thought teach players to maintain a single point of view throughout a scene, indeed to resist change altogether. While this may work well when playing a certain type of shortform, be aware that it becomes problematic in longform.

There are thousands of rich, nuanced, complex characters in scripted work, and such characters seldom emerge through improvisation when held back by limitations in content, direction and playing style. The changes that Malvolio is forced to undergo in *Twelfth Night* are the source of much humour (albeit cruel). The comedy in *A Midsummer Night's Dream* depends on subversion, upheaval of the status quo, and characters undergoing significant change, before order (of a sort) is eventually restored. While driving a single point of view can provide intensity and clarity of focus, don't let it limit you.

Characteristics can be discovered by pursuing a single point of view, but *character* will be revealed through change.

Whether you are improvising as a hobby or a profession, truthful behaviour and connection with others is going to make your scenes watchable. Your work (and the work of those around you) will be richer for it.

Multiple Players

Adding more players to a scene becomes exponentially difficult. The chances of missed beats, clashing ideas, talking over each other or pulling in different directions all increase. More attention will be given to focus and staging later in this book, but in order to keep any scene involving multiple players clear and presentable, it is essential to know whose scene it is and where the focus of each player should be.

With three or more players, consider the status differences between the characters. This helps not only to differentiate them but also to provide clarity of focus in the scene.

Scenes and stories often benefit from 'drop-ins', characters who fulfil whatever function is required to keep the scene moving forward. If the scene takes place in a bar, then a bartender might be required or a waiter may be needed to drop in during a café scene. These scenes are not about the bartender or waiter, although they can still be delightful and entertaining characters. The discipline is to know what function the character serves and how it contributes to the forward movement or setting of the scene.

Revisit the endowment games for ways to begin three-player scenes (pages 96 and 97).

The Audience

At some point you are going to want to get out of the class, rehearsal room or workshop, and perform to an audience.

While studying, your classmates have been your audience and whatever your experience has been of that dynamic, it is about to evolve.

In fact, the role of the audience, utterly vital to improvised performance, is woefully underexplored in tuition. Sadly, this is increasingly endemic; improv, when performed without an understanding of actor–audience dynamic, can become self-referential, indulgent and tedious. I have witnessed intolerably dull presentations justified because the performers were 'trying a new format', about which the audience knew nothing. I have been baffled by groups that dutifully execute their 'sweeps' and 'tags' (methods used to edit scenes and switch players during performance) without being able to engage their audience *at all*, endorsing a perception that improv is a hobby for its performers more than a form of storytelling designed for audience enjoyment.

An audience at an improv performance, knowing the entertainment to be unscripted, has particular expectations and appreciations. They find it easier to identify and value *risk*; they understand that there is greater potential for volatility (that anything could happen); they may seek proof that the event is spontaneous (and some will feel cheated if they become suspicious); they want agency and influence (contributing suggestions to the performers, for example); they are more tolerant of things not working (for a while at least); they reward effort and bravery; they marvel more easily; they love it when the performer is in trouble; they laugh at moments that often would not elicit laughter were the same moment to appear in a rehearsed play; they may be more willing to participate vocally; and they have a completely different investment in, and attachment to, the outcome of the event.

Showstopper! The Improvised Musical asks the audience for some information at the start of the show: Where is this musical set? What other musicals have influenced it? What is it called? Having played the show more than a thousand times across different countries, I have observed some commonalities in audience behaviour:

1. They are generally up for a good time.

2. They are excited to see their idea immediately come to life on stage. They are also pleased when an idea has been suggested, left unexplored for a while, then reincorporated when they have forgotten about it.

3. There are always people who want to set the show in a toilet, usually because they think it will be funny to cheapen the experience. Other common suggestions include the moon, a supermarket or fast-food outlet, maybe because they are places that feel removed from the language of the typical musical, and therefore subversive choices.

4. There are always suggestions in shockingly poor taste (which we avoid), such as war zones, serial killers and other areas of human suffering. Again, the desire behind making such suggestions publicly is to shock, subvert and impress.

5. With a small amount of encouragement, audiences are happy to think more ambitiously.

6. Many audiences want to see a musical set in their area or locale, reflecting their community.

7. If the execution of the presentation is too slick, some people cannot believe it is improvised. Rather than downgrade the quality of the work to remedy this,

Showstopper! adamantly continued to raise the bar. As such, we found that our 'writer' character – who collects all the audience suggestions at the beginning of the show – could be used throughout the show, affording us opportunities to refer continually to the audience and invest in their ideas.

The Die-Nasty players like to get laughs (and they get plenty), but they know it is harder to make an audience cry when improvising, and harder still to provoke a gasp. Audiences may be generous with their laughter, and sometimes tears too, but they will never fake a gasp.

Audiences tend to be more vocal in improv, where integration of ideas between performer and audience is encouraged, certainly at the top of the show, and sometimes throughout. It's important that performers attune to this immediacy of feedback. What kind of laugh was that? A warm laugh? A nervous laugh? A weary laugh? A growing realisation? Clowns attune to these responses, allowing the audience to direct them. Improvisers must develop the same kind of radar because the scene or story is being discovered and shaped live in the moment. Listening to and understanding audience reaction is essential.

Some improv presentations require the performer to talk directly to the audience – monologues, narrations and asides, for example. While some actors' eyes glaze over as they talk generally into the darkness, specific relationships with individual members of the audience can instead be established. Stand-up comics talk about finding their 'best friend' and their 'worst critic' in the crowd. Who seems to like you? Who appears cold and detached? And how does that, in turn, affect you? Engage your audience both en masse and as individuals.

Playing the Faces

Another game learned from Ken Campbell while we prepared for our *Shall We Shog?* show at Shakespeare's Globe. This can work with an improvised speech but is best suited to a speech that has been memorised. Shakespearean soliloquies are perfect because they were written to be played to an audience seen clearly in daylight.

The actor stands in front of the audience and, starting with one person they see in the crowd, mirrors their facial expression and begins the speech. At any time the actor can move on to another audience member, observing and changing to copy this new facial expression. Each change affects the speech in ways that constantly surprise the performer. Playing the faces encourages:

- Two-way communication resulting from direct, specific audience engagement.
- Yielding any attachment to the speech and its delivery.
- The performer to be directed by the audience.
- The performer to embrace unexpected change.

When we played *Soundball* at the very start of our training (page 41) we were learning to let the new sound affect and change us. When we played with three soundballs we had to check that our offer reached its target. When addressing the audience directly, watch to see how your offers are affecting them.

You are never alone on stage. What, one might ask, would be the point?

Set-ups

Most improv shows have some sort of set-up/introduction at the start. Sometimes to contextualise the entertainment, sometimes to warm up the audience and develop a rapport, sometimes to get information or suggestions that will influence the action.

Many shows open with the question: 'Who here has never been to an improv show before?'

Why?

What does this achieve?

Most people aren't keen to share anything that might feel like ignorance, and some people do not wish to have attention drawn to them in an audience. The question creates awkwardness in the room. Furthermore, what do the performers do with this information? From my observations, absolutely nothing of any relevance at all. If you are going to open a show by talking with the audience, work out precisely why. What is the function of the opening address or exchange?

Showstopper! opens with a red 'hotline' telephone ringing. A big producer is calling the offices of Showstopper Productions because they need a new musical – and fast. Our writer, who also acts as compère for the evening, pitches a brand-new musical to the producer by enlisting the audience's help. 'No problem,' says the writer, 'I have my musical-theatre experts with me.' The audience is endowed as a musical-theatre focus group, whose help and expertise is desperately needed. The writer then asks the audience for the setting, song styles, and finally a title. And away we go. These initial eight minutes are vitally important: the opening contextualises the show, giving the audience status and agency; it creates a sense of collective ambition as the writer goads them into 'dreaming big'; it warms them up and gets them used to the idea that they can call out suggestions that will influence the action; it raises the bar as to expectation of quality (after all, we have to impress a leading producer); and it creates a sense of mischief that we are all in this together, pitting our wits against our imaginary impresario. We don't need to know how many in our audience have been to an improv show before.

In *The Society of Strange* the company improvises *weird tales*, stories of the strange, sinister and downright disturbing. The show begins eerily with the slow entrance of three travelling players, as if arriving in the space for the first time. The players put down their suitcases, turn to the audience, quote some H. P. Lovecraft, explain that there will be three stories, and then ask the audience to point at the actor they want to play the leading role in the first tale. The silent pointing feels creepy and there is often nervous laughter, all of which helps to establish the mood and tone of the show right from the start.

In *Rhapsodes* we spend a couple of minutes interviewing a volunteer from the audience about one of their ancestors. When were they alive? What was their occupation? Were there any curious incidents associated with them? This 'bullet-point life story' forms the inspiration for an entire Shakespearean-style play. Have faith in your audience. With a little encouragement they will move past the knee-jerk desire to shock or subvert. Every one of the many such interviews we have conducted in *Rhapsodes* over the years has resulted in fascinating, surprising and nuanced material for us to work with.

In *Mischief Movie Night* we are introduced to the whole company in a high-energy entrance before a character called Oscar talks with the audience, claiming to have a video library of 'every film you could ever imagine'. The question is, what film do you want to watch today? Oscar collects the genre of film, the opening location, a title, an audience member's 'favourite moment' and often some other ideas too (e.g. a musical number, a scene directed by a famous director). The goader-rhapsode model here facilitates numerous games between Oscar and the cast of the onstage movie.

In comedic presentations, performers like to talk with the audience, keeping things light and getting a feel for what kind of crowd they are playing with.

Whether punk-casual with beer in hand or daringly theatrical with ambitious production values, consider what your connection to the audience is and how you would like the audience to listen.

What should you ask for?

Whether you aim to get one word to inspire a longform show or prefer to re-engage the audience for further offers throughout, you are going to have to know exactly what you are asking for and why. Longformers embarking on a Harold, for example, can go with pretty much any single-word offer from the audience, probably only rejecting suggestions if they are in bad taste. For those groups repeatedly asking the audience for offers, a number of questions must be confronted:

Will you take the first suggestion?

Practice will help you know whether a suggestion is helpful, in that it provokes good comedy/drama, or unhelpful, in that it probably won't. Many suggestions are offered without much thought for what the ensuing scene might look like. You are not obliged to take the first suggestion. You can 'haggle' for a better one. All that matters is you are cultivating conditions for great entertainment.

Grand Theft Impro's anarchic Drew Levy once asked: 'What are my hands made of?' and subsequently played a character with potatoes on the ends of his arms.

Audience suggestions designed to subvert expectations often turn out to be dull or tasteless. You don't have to take them. I once saw an improviser warmly engage the crowd and, after being given a suggestion he didn't like, charmingly dismiss it by replying: 'That's a great suggestion – now let's have another great suggestion!' Alternatively, The Noise Next Door like to play fast and furiously, taking the first suggestion they hear, getting into the scene or game as swiftly as possible.

Why are you asking the audience at all?

American improv duo TJ and Dave famously begin their shows without asking for anything from the audience, instead ending their introductions with: 'Trust us, this is all improvised.'

If you want a lever or stimulus for the imagination, you might want to spend more time refining what you ask the audience for. In shortform, common asks include a setting for the scene (e.g. a gift shop or a graveyard) or a relationship between the characters (e.g. siblings or old flames). These work well because the audience clearly sees how the suggestion influences the action.

In *Theatresports*™, which is especially popular in Canada and some parts of Europe, teams in mock-competition challenge each other to play scenes, which are then scored by a panel of judges. The scoring, and indeed most aspects of *Theatresports*™, is more for show than accuracy. A typical challenge might be:

- We challenge you to play a scene involving music.
- We challenge you to speak in one voice.
- We challenge you to play a scene with audience participation.
- We challenge you to play something topical.
- We challenge you to a scene without words.

Challenges can be anything. However, each team might want to ask the audience for something before they start, to give their take on the challenge a different slant, e.g. 'What is my character's occupation in this scene without words?'

The opening of a show sets the tone for how the audience will engage with the event. There is an implicit tension in the fact that it is improvised. Will it work? Will the players fall off the highwire? Do you want to put the audience at ease? If so, how? I assert that 'Who here has never been to an improv show before?' is not necessarily the way to do that. Do you want to play on that sense of unease? Or have you noticed there is no unease in the room tonight? Do the audience need warming up or settling down? How quickly can you gauge the mood in the room, and to what degree do you want to address it?

There are details in improv presentations that are carbon-copied by other groups without understanding. Inevitably the result is distracting and undermines the performance. Longform often plays with a 'backline', a row of performers standing upstage watching the action while waiting to engage in scenes. Unless performers make this backline integral to their design and play with theatrical discipline, many audiences find it upstaging and distracting. The set of *Showstopper!* allows the performers to exit but still be able to watch the action from behind an upstage screen with see-through gauze panels. This encourages the actors to make entrances and exits as you would expect to see in a musical. Think about what you are presenting to the audience and what effect it might have on them. To neglect this is to indulge in your craft rather than refine it.

In shortform improv the audience often directly affects the action with frequent intervention for suggestions. In *Showstopper!* the writer/MC asks the audience to vote on vital plot moments, for example: 'Does he run away from town?', 'Does she accept the promotion?' The story can go in any direction and the audience understands it has a degree of agency.

Further Observations

Get out of your head

If you have studied improv you may at some stage have heard someone tell you to 'get out of your head'. It's an absurdly unhelpful piece of coaching and I have only ever seen it compound the problem, since the performer gets more tense while pretending not to be.

This direction is usually given when a performer is caught thinking about something or processing something in such a way that it is detrimental to their immediacy. The performer has detached or disconnected from the moment and we, the audience, are now given reason to disengage with them.

Jill Bernard offers the most simple and effective advice on the subject: 'If you don't want to be in your head, be somewhere else.'

Outward focus is the key to all effective acting.

There is nothing wrong with thinking. You can't help but think. You are a living, breathing, thinking, feeling being. It's natural. It can, in fact, be very engaging to watch someone thinking, processing, figuring things out. It only becomes problematic when the audience senses the performer's uncertainty. If this happens to you, place your attention on someone else, or anywhere outside of yourself – such as a task or activity. Play the *'You Look...'* exercise (page 90) in the middle of a scene to reconnect with your fellow players.

Talking from the subconscious

When the improviser is tense or anxious about the scene they are in, sometimes their subconscious thoughts are given voice and begin directing the scene. I ask improvisers not only to listen to others *but to listen to what they themselves are saying.* This manifests itself both in the voice and in the body. Here are some examples from narrative improv shows I have seen presented by inexperienced players:

- Well, this wasn't my idea.
- Why can't we all come together as a team?
- Look, let's just forget about this and move on.
- I'm scared because this isn't working.
- I thought I could do this but I don't know what I'm doing.

In each instance, this dialogue occurred when the plot became entangled and the performers had become visibly tense and unhappy with the situation they found themselves in, collectively struggling to know what to do about it. The words seemingly emanated from the characters, but was actually an expression of the improvisers' anxieties. Fear, blame and insecurity start to spill out of the improvisers and onto the stage in the guise of dramatic action.

The same happens with the body. You will observe performers who say one thing while their body completely contradicts them. Examples I have seen in improvisation include:

- 'But I love you. I long for you!' – *while the body is awkwardly pulling in the opposite direction.*
- 'How dare you, I'm going to kill you!' – *while the body is limp and devoid of energy.*

This is very common when miming activity. As with most things on stage, miming benefits from commitment and specificity. As the performer loses faith in the scene or their role within it, the activity becomes completely detached and disconnected. Painting a fence becomes vaguely waving hands in the air. Building a car resembles moving small boxes around without purpose.

Your physicality affects you. The more affected you are by what's happening around you, the easier it is to improvise. You are creating less and reacting more.

Stuck?

Yes. There's a lot to think about. But you don't have to think about it all at once. In fact, I recommend not doing so.

I remember learning to play the piano when I was young. There were sequences I couldn't master and I would thump the keys in frustration. Learning takes time. You are unlikely to be expected to play the 'Rach Three' (Sergei Rachmaninoff's Piano Concerto No. 3 in D minor, Op. 30) after only a year of piano training.

Have a look at what's troubling you. Break it down into small, manageable components.

If you are playing a scene while worrying about endowment, status, investing in the environment, reincorporation, being affected by your scene partner, then you will remain just that – worried.

This is why the Karate Kid had to spend weeks waxing on and waxing off.

Keep practising. Everything improves with repetition, discipline and diligence.

Meanwhile, if you are playing scenes either in class or in shows and you feel stuck, here are some things you can try:

1. Outward focus

As a director and acting coach, I would say that seventy per cent of the time when actors tell me they are having a problem in a scene, it can be distilled to the same single thing: the actor isn't putting the focus of their attention on someone, or something, else. They have become self-conscious, self-absorbed, worried. Their inner monologue is haranguing them.

Focus outward. Focus on your scene partner and try to change the expression on their face.

(Since you ask, fifteen per cent of the time, the problem is that the actor is trying to play a number of things at once, when they would more effectively play a single beat or action at a time, and the remaining fifteen per cent of the time is because of some technical problem specific to the text, set or costume.)

2. Slow down

Why are you rushing? Look at what's around you – the other players, the environment. Take a moment and just be where you are. It's okay. We'll wait.

3. Don't worry if it isn't funny

Even quickfire comedy suffers when players force the funny. Remember you aren't the only player (and even if you start alone on stage, others can come in to help you out), so you can play straight and facilitate someone else being funny. Or realise this isn't the funny bit. And if you aren't appearing in a comedy show, don't *ever* worry about being funny.

In my early days improvising I played with a group of very experienced, fast and funny players in Canada. I told myself: 'I'm not the funny one here,' and calmed down. I learned how to connect with them and play scenes, and soon not only was I helping them to be funny, but I also started finding my own funny moments.

I remind myself of this all the time.

You are not boring if you are being truthful. Bertolt Brecht once said: 'There is nothing so interesting in life as watching a man trying to get a knot out of his shoelaces.'

4. *Make a change*

Do something different. Do something random. You won't 'break' improv. You might open up a new direction, game or idea. Try it. Try it even when you don't need to and see what happens. Or try to break a scene in rehearsal. See how hard you have to work to destroy something. It might turn out to be harder than you thought, and you might discover something wonderful.

5. *Personal meaning*

It's always good to make things matter to you personally. The stakes are higher when it means something. Again, beware of glibness. The watch owned by Butch (Bruce Willis) in *Pulp Fiction* has one heck of a story behind it and its personal meaning propels Butch into danger. When Hamlet learns that the skull he is holding is Yorick's, the scene changes completely (Act Five, Scene One).

If you are struggling in a scene it might be because nothing means enough to you. If the game you are playing isn't compelling enough, you are going to need to invest in meaning. This applies to comedy as much as any other form of drama. John Cleese's Basil Fawlty invests so much in his lucky winnings on a horse ('for the first time in my life I'm winning') that it drives him to hilarious and agonising destruction.

If you are struggling with this, try using an *Overaccept* (page 122). Have a big emotional reaction to something without knowing why: 'What? We've run out of grapes?? How could you say that? How dare you?!' Commit to your choice once made and play as passionately and as truthfully as you can.

6. Say 'There's something I've been meaning to tell you...'

You don't need to know what comes next. Allow it to surprise you.

7. Say 'I love you'

Seriously. Try it.

8. Work with what authentically is

Feeling vulnerable in real life? Be vulnerable in the scene. Feeling angry and don't know why? That's a genuine impulse. Be angry. Is your scene partner confusing you? Tell them you find them confusing. You don't have to be reasonable and polite all the time. Exciting actors are *volatile* and *vulnerable*. I once worked with an actor about to do a twenty-four-hour improvised show with his group. He said he didn't always feel part of the group and felt they often didn't understand him. He was concerned that he would upset or offend them in the show and he asked me what I thought he could do. I suggested he play a character who was very concerned not to offend anyone and that he should study people carefully to see if he was offending them. Work with what *is*. Be where you are. The moment you are in now is ephemeral. It will soon lead you to the next moment, and the next, until suddenly... you find yourself somewhere else.

9. It doesn't always work

Tina Fey and Amy Poehler famously said: 'We've done thousands of scenes together and do you know five or six of them were really rather good.'

Some things will remain a mystery. Thankfully.

10. Get off the stage

You can always leave. Another scene will be coming along soon enough…

◊ ◊ ◊

Hone your skills in the classroom or workshop as if working out in a gym. Try focusing on different skills in isolation. You can make a list if it's helpful.

Today I'll…

- practise endowment.
- play games to help me feel more confident with specificity.
- play more low-status characters.
- push myself to go on stage when I don't have an idea.
- experiment with faster tempos.

…and so on.

In performance, allow all of this to fall back into your muscle memory, keep it simple, and focus outwardly. You want to be in the moment – not several other moments.

If it all becomes overwhelming, wax on, wax off, and focus on those basic principles:

- *Listen* – Be outwardly focused, interested in others and willing to be changed.
- *Accept* – Play games with people and allow yourself to be affected by others.
- *Commit* – Go for it!

And remember – there is no such thing as a mistake.

Summary

Connect

Play one beat at a time.

Keep ideas connected with simple, obvious choices.

Surprise and subversion can come later.

Discover patterns during play.

Scene Shape

Platform – development – reincorporation.

Invest in your environment.

A scene has continual forward movement.

Techniques

Be specific!

Activity can be symbolic, literal or contrasting.

Emotional development – something has to matter.

Look for status behavioural indicators.

Character and characteristics.

Learn to understand and work with the actor–audience dynamic.

4.

The Story

So far we have been examining the principles that allow performers to be authentically in the moment, and considering how to connect these moments in order to build scenes. Now we will look at how scenes connect in order to form *story* and *plot*.

Story is what happens – a series of connected events:

- Macbeth is given a prophecy that he will become king.
- He shares this news with his wife.
- He kills the king.

Plot is how the audience discover it happening – the causality of events:

- Macbeth kills the king *because* of the witches' prophecy and his wife's encouragement.

If you want to improvise a narrative, I recommend you think less about the techniques of improvisation for a moment and address the actual subject of *story*. Want to know what boxing is like? Get in the ring. Want to know about singing? Sing a song. There are no short cuts or cheats. You need to know about story.

The good news is that you already know quite a lot.

Kids have a great understanding of story. They are immersed in storytelling. Story is in our DNA. It's how we interpret and comprehend the world. So trust that you already know a lot about story. You've read books, seen films, listened to songs, played video games, been to the theatre, watched dramas, comedies, soap operas and stories in many different forms across multiple genres. It's all there, just as you will have picked up some musicality by listening to lots of music throughout your life. Trust it.

When you watch a James Bond film and see Q showing Bond all those gadgets, you expect them to reappear later in the film, otherwise you would leave the cinema asking: 'But what about the ejector-seat in that car? We never saw it again.' Having been established, the gadget should be used.

Writer Anton Chekhov said if you show a gun in Act One, it must be used in Act Two or Three (rail against Chekhov if you want, but he was a master craftsman).[15] The principle being that a theme or motif in the development of a narrative is more satisfying if it has already been seeded earlier. Time taken in the early part of an improvised story to give something significance will reap rewards later on.

Ideally, Bond's gadget is used at a critical moment and at a time when you, the viewer, have forgotten about it. As screenwriter William Goldman puts it: 'Give the audience what it wants, but not the way it expects.'[16]

You know about reincorporation in storytelling. It can be found in fairytales and the stories you grew up with. It's in your bones. The reincorporation can be of an object, an event, emotion, theme... pretty much anything.

15. Guns in general, as those of you who have seen Michael Scott in his improv class (in *The Office: An American Workplace*) will know, are as problematic as they are ubiquitous in improv.
16. Robert McKee (quoting William Goldman), *Story: Substance, Structure, Style and the Principles of Screenwriting*, Methuen, 1999.

You also know that, in order for a story to be satisfying, the scenes must connect in some way. Try telling a story to a child where nothing connects, where the characters don't develop and changes are random, and, after a while, they will call for the story to find form.

In *The Showstoppers' Kids Show*, which is primarily aimed at families with children aged four to ten years old, we constantly ask the children what happens next. The actors try to make very few, if any, plot decisions and let the audience control the entire story. Over the years, we have learned a great deal from children as storytellers:

- They have a love of silliness, subversion and transgression.

- They like the middle section of the story to break down, fall apart and be anarchic.

- They like to put the characters in trouble and have them make mistakes.

- They want the story to make sense in the end.

- They always reincorporate characters and ideas in the final third of the story.

At the end of the show the kids are invited on stage to draw their favourite moments. We can very quickly tell from the quality of these drawings how effective we have been as a group of storytellers. The more detail given to the characters and representation of key moments, the more engaged our young audience must have been.

So there are some basic principles for improvised storytelling that you already know:

- Keep ideas and events connected.

- Keep the action moving forward.

- Allow characters to develop, change and have significant experiences.

- Reincorporate.

When improvisers begin to engage in narrative work they often lose all the wonderful freedom they discovered and practised while playing games or scenes in isolation. They start to worry again about 'getting it right'. They worry that a certain choice will ruin or undermine the story, or they over-compensate and play boldly without connection, having no understanding of why their choices might be unhelpful. The performer ceases to be in the moment, stops observing and responding to what is around them, and disconnects, attempting to become a *writer shaping a story* rather than a *performer experiencing the story from within*. As my fellow Showstopper Philip Pellew suggests: 'We are not *telling* a story so much as *making* one.' Audiences enjoy seeing us construct it from the inside.

In the same way beginner improvisers in a scene tend to argue because they think it makes interesting drama, the novice storyteller feels pressure to come up with big story choices and developments. In this anxious state they begin to resist change. They are thinking about what to do next (or what not to do) rather than playing freely. They start trying to tell the whole story rather than one beat of it. Remind them of the word-at-a-time-story exercises (page 53) and *Sandwiches* (page 43), in which they can contribute only a single connected beat at any given moment. Revisit these games often as you branch out into exploring story.

Players are also quick to create situations of crisis and emergency because, as with individual scenes, they worry that the audience will be bored if they don't.

But audiences seldom tire of truthful behaviour and they enjoy watching the interaction of people they care about.

Characters affecting each other and undergoing change can be all the story you need. You don't have to run on stage breathlessly and say that war has been declared or that someone has fallen down the well.

So, to start with, stop worrying about plot and story.

While developing *Showstopper!* in the rehearsal room I initiated an exercise in which we improvised a musical, but if at any point we 'smelled the plot' I rang the bell, the show was over and we had to start a new one. The challenge was to see how long we could keep going as a company and still maintain interest in the narrative without resorting to external plot calls or sudden crisis/emergency. Some beautiful, nuanced storytelling emerged, and it was always entertaining when somebody accidentally pushed the plot too hard and I was forced to ring the bell.

We also explored the opposite end of this spectrum and developed a type of performer called 'Fiery Joe' – an improviser who is locked into story-mode and bombards other players with far too much plot. The idea of the game is that everyone else has to adapt to Joe and somehow make the scene work. Note that the aim isn't to ignore or negate Fiery Joe, but to work *with* Joe, to allow the chaotic plot-attack to affect the other players in order for it to become significant and meaningful. The more the cast embraced Fiery Joe, the less 'fiery' Joe inevitably became.

The gentler approach doesn't work for all occasions. Some stories require bold decisions and more dramatic plot movement. This brings up numerous challenges to the individual and group alike.

In life, our decisions have consequences, which is why we often prevaricate and agonise over making them. But in improvisation, the only consequence of these decisions is *drama*.

Players often avoid all the dangers of a scene or a story because they are used to guarding against consequence. It would be like watching Hamlet kicking around with his mates at university but never seeing him argue with his mother, ensnare Claudius with a play, or duel with Laertes.

Character, as we have already seen, is habitual action, the choices we repeatedly make and the choices we make under pressure. These choices are how story develops and how character emerges. So make a decision. Even better, make a bad one so that your character can suffer the consequences.

Trust that you already know more about story than you may think.

A Beginning, a Middle and an End

A scene, as John Yorke observes in his book *Into the Woods*, is a story in microcosm. The first part of the scene establishes the characters, the scenario and the premise. The second part is a development where characters go 'Into the Woods' (i.e. into the unknown). The third part is some kind of resolution – not necessarily a neat one (it may, in all likelihood, lead to another scene), but certainly a conclusion to that unit of dramatic action.

In our study of scene construction so far we have come to know this as:

- Platform
- Development
- Reincorporation

A Beginning, a Middle, and an End.

This three-part structure is ubiquitous in storytelling. Classic fairytales often unfold in three units: *Goldilocks and the Three*

Bears, The Three Little Pigs, Three Billy Goats Gruff. Note also in such stories the prevalence of three wishes, three tasks, or three attempts to guess Rumplestiltskin's name. Jokes, too, frequently rely upon three beats, often structured around three characters, the punchline usually arriving with the action of the third character.

Three is a powerful number in narrative work. It is the shortest number of beats possible to create a pattern and then break or subvert it (two beats to suggest a pattern before it can be changed in the third beat).

When examining story in improvisation I tend to start with three 'chapters', for example…

Macbeth

Chapter One – Macbeth, a Scottish soldier, meets three witches who prophesy that he will become Thane of Cawdor and eventually King. The witches also declare that Macbeth's friend, Banquo, will have children who will become kings. Following his bravery in battle, Macbeth is promoted to the rank of Thane of Cawdor by King Duncan, just as the witches predicted. Macbeth's wife persuades him that he should now set his sights on becoming King.

Chapter Two – Macbeth, persuaded and assisted by his wife, secretly murders King Duncan and is crowned King of Scotland. Duncan's sons flee to England, thereby making them appear responsible for the crime. But Macbeth begins to fear his position is insecure and that Banquo's son, Fleance, may take his throne as foretold by the witches. Macbeth's attempts to kill Fleance fail and, after having Banquo murdered, he is haunted by Banquo's ghost.

Chapter Three – Those wronged by Macbeth rally together to defeat him. Lady Macbeth, driven mad with guilt, dies. The witches predict Macbeth's end and, although he fights to the last, he is eventually vanquished. Order is restored and Malcolm is to be crowned King of Scotland.

Legally Blonde (the musical)

Chapter One – Bubbly, blonde sorority president Elle Woods is expecting her boyfriend, Warner, to propose to her at a romantic dinner. But when Warner explains he is going to study law at Harvard and needs to be with someone more serious, he breaks up with her. Elle is devastated and decides she must study law and follow him to Harvard to win him back.

Chapter Two – Life at Harvard is tough for Elle, who is frequently ridiculed, and she only makes one friend, Emmett. Elle becomes a brunette to appear more serious, but suffers a string of humiliations, including seeing Warner propose to someone else and an unwanted advance from her law professor.

Chapter Three – Elle, seemingly against the odds, becomes an excellent lawyer, winning a major case, finding her true strengths, and eventually proposing to Emmett.

You should be able to take almost any story and divide it into three simple stages as above.

- *Chapter One* – A status quo that eventually changes. A premise.

- *Chapter Two* – An exploration of the premise with maximum possible drama for the characters.

- *Chapter Three* – Reincorporation of earlier ideas to reach some form of conclusion.

Three Chapters

Starting with two actors, and have them play a complete story in three scenes.

- *The Beginning* – Establish the characters, their relationship, their setting, and a premise.

- *The Middle* – A development of the premise, putting heat under what matters and allowing characters to be affected and changed by their interaction.

- *The End* – Use reincorporation to find a resolution.

There is no way of knowing how long each scene will be, although you can play with time constraints if you wish (e.g. each scene must be three minutes long). Such restrictions can be good practice, but look out for the tensions that time limitations can cause.

Each scene can segue into the next, or time can pass between each scene. It depends on the actors' choices as they feel their way through the story. The only rule the exercise is that there should be precisely three scenes in the story.

An example Three Chapters *scenario*

Two improvisers begin with the *'You Look…'* exercise (page 90), relate through observation, and discover the following scenario:

- *The Beginning* – Chandra and Max are two housemates in their early twenties, throwing a housewarming party in their new home. Max is anxious – he would love to meet someone romantically but his obsession with order and cleanliness means he is frightened that the party will mess up the house. He's actually thinking of cancelling altogether. His housemate, Chandra, has had a rough few weeks and is looking for an excuse to let her hair down. Besides, she wants to show off the new house to her friends, especially a piano which has been in her family for years and is now hers. She reminds Max that 'fortune favours the brave', and his last-minute wobble is allayed just before the doorbell rings and the first guest arrives.

- *The Middle* – The actors initiate a time-jump, and this scene takes place in Max's bedroom, five hours later. The party is in full swing but our two characters have isolated themselves because their guests are getting out of control. Max is interested in a girl named Annika and therefore is less concerned about the increasingly wild party. Chandra, however, has changed her mind. She is scared that her possessions are going to be damaged – especially the piano. The whole thing has been a terrible mistake. How are they going to get their guests to leave? Chandra calls the police, pretending to be a neighbour, reporting them for the noise. Max is furious because ending the party might also end his chances of being with Annika.

- *The End* – Another time-jump as we pick up the action early the next morning. Chandra is appalled to see so many of her possessions damaged, but Max is thrilled to find a note from Annika with her phone number on it, stapled to Chandra's piano. He decides they should throw another party. 'Fortune favours the brave,' he says, reminding Chandra of her own advice as they tidy up the mess and restore order to their house.

The Beginning showed two characters *joining* in activity but *contrasting* in their points of view. Chandra is excited about the party, Max is anxious, but they both set up and prepare for the arrival of their guests. Note that Max's *resistance* does not interfere with the *forward movement* of the scene. Max discovers that he has an *intention* – he'd love to meet a girl – while Chandra is looking to let her hair down.

The Middle sees a development of the key ideas, *putting heat under what is already there.* Max wanted to meet someone, but the wild party has forced him to retreat to his bedroom. Chandra, who wanted to host a party more than Max did, is now regretting her decision. Both of them are going 'into the woods'.

The End uses reincorporation of ideas and themes. The reincorporation of 'fortune favours the brave' and the piano help give this short story a sense of conclusion. Most importantly, our characters have developed and changed. Max has hope where before he had none, while Chandra, who so wanted the party in the first place, has suffered for her recklessness. Max no longer cares that the house is wrecked because Annika's interest in him is more important. It's Chandra who now cares about the mess and regrets her actions. This kind of reversal is common to many stories with two protagonists.

At any given moment there are myriad possibilities as to where the story could go. In the middle section of the above example there are numerous ways to put heat under the premise: Max might make a fool of himself romantically and experience further rejection, or he might get so drunk and lonely that he makes a clumsy pass at Chandra, whereas Chandra could become more reckless, damaging her beloved possessions herself, or trying to set up a romantic attachment for Max. As you think about this story you will no doubt come up with many ideas yourself. At this stage keep the ideas within a circle of expectation. Develop the premise that has already been suggested. Put heat under what is already there.

But can't I make surprising choices?

Sure – but draw like da Vinci before you paint like Picasso.

Any of the improvisers can make offers, decisions and endowments that shape the overall story. Players can enter scenes at any time to add to, and develop, the narrative. The lighting operator can affect the story by deciding a scene is over and moving the players on to the next one. A musician can suggest something has importance by adding underscoring. Everyone in the event can contribute. Anything made explicit in any way becomes woven into the fabric of the story.

The *London Improvathon* uses a director to call the start of each scene, explaining which characters are in the scene and where the scene takes place, and often offering some suggestion as to the premise of the scene. The actors then further the scene by developing it in any way they may discover. Direction, in this case, is a stimulus or springboard for content, for example: 'Rex and Cathy meet in the bar and the past soon catches up with them.'

Here the director is suggesting that the characters have history, but exactly what kind of backstory is up to the actors. As Rex and Cathy explore what their past was and what it means to them now, the director can take notes, which may become relevant when calling future scenes for these characters.

Three Chapters in Any Sequence

Once you have become more practised at playing three scenes you can play them out of sequence. There are now six possibilities:

1. Middle – End – Beginning
2. Middle – Beginning – End
3. End – Middle – Beginning

4. End – Beginning – Middle

5. Beginning – End – Middle

6. Beginning – Middle – End

Playing three-scene stories out of sequence throws up all sorts of possibilities and helps performers engage with story principles.

You can practise the *Three Chapters* exercises with three specified areas of the stage representing Beginning, Middle and End so that everyone knows which part of the story you are walking into (e.g. 'Ah, they're playing the scene centre-stage, so they must be starting in the Middle' or 'Stage-left represents the End scene'), or you can play all three scenes in the centre of the stage and let the players discover whether their scene is a Beginning, a Middle or an End.

You can increase the number of players, although I recommend starting with two and building up practice and experience before doing so.

You can play with six actors, keeping the same two characters throughout but switching the performers playing those characters in each scene. This is an effective tool for keeping the whole group focused on the same story.

You can develop this exercise as you wish with any number of players, extras, drop-ins, moving locations, switching characters, music, adding songs, exploring linear and non-linear time, etc.

Make sure you maintain the discipline of telling one story in three scenes.

An example Three Chapters in Any Sequence *scenario*

- Scene One (*Middle*) – Anya and Tony are exchanging wedding vows.

- Scene Two (*Beginning*) – Anya and Tony meet.

- Scene Three (*End*) – Anya and Tony meet again years later after their divorce.

In observing that Scene One is a marriage between two characters, the actors have a choice as to where to place that scene in the overall narrative. Is the wedding the Beginning, the Middle, or the End of the story? Of course, it can be any of these options – all that matters is where the players place the next scene. If the next scene is the honeymoon, how does that affect Scene One? Is the honeymoon the Middle or the End? It all depends upon the *content* of both the wedding scene and the honeymoon scene.

So it might play differently, as follows:

- *Scene One* – Anya and Tony are exchanging wedding vows. It is the climax of their happiness. The actors are not using the scene to build a platform or establish characters, they are assuming that we already know about these characters and that we are therefore joining them later along the line of their journey.

- *Scene Two* – Having paid attention to the content of Scene One, the actors now play the honeymoon scene as if it were a perfect resolution to the whole story. This decision makes this second scene the End scene, and contextualises the wedding (the first scene) as now being the Middle scene.

- *Scene Three* – As the first scene was the Middle and the second scene was the End, all that is left now is to play a scene set *before* the wedding. Seeing as the honeymoon was quite close to the wedding, it makes sense to keep this scene chronologically quite close to the wedding as well. The actors play the night before the wedding, with the groom and bride on the phone to each other, completing their wedding plans, talking about guests, family, their excitement and anticipation.

The sequence, therefore, is now completed as 'Middle – End – Beginning'.

Three-Sentence Story

For quick practice, create stories using three sentences only. It can be played with three actors, each offering one sentence. For example:

A. Once upon a time there was a greedy tyrant who wanted all the wealth she could muster, even though her mother always told her that happiness lay in simplicity and purity.

B. She stole as much as she could from the people of her village but was never sated.

C. She was eventually overthrown by the people and put in prison, where she learned that simplicity and purity were indeed the key to happiness, and she thanked the spirit of her mother.

Or:

A. In Paris during the Second World War a telephone-exchange operator joins the French Resistance.

B. Using the telephone exchange she discovers her husband is a collaborator and that they are on opposite sides of the conflict, but she decides not to betray him.

C. After the war she discovers that he was a double agent who was secretly working for her side after all.

Or:

A. Teenager Val is sick of the household chores her overbearing aunt and uncle make her do while she is living with them in the country.

B. She runs away from them and joins a travelling theatre company, playing all over the world.

C. On her final performance she sees her aunt and uncle in the audience. All is forgiven as they are reunited at last.

You may notice that, in order for these stories to feel complete, reincorporation of characters and ideas in the third sentence is essential. In the tale of teenager Val, the last sentence could read: 'She was a successful actor who lived very happily for the rest of her days' – which is good for Val but doesn't make for a satisfying story. The return of the aunt and uncle and the resolution of their emotional differences is vital.

Try three-sentence stories in different genres. Experiment with a ghost story, a romantic comedy or a historical epic. You will find that genres require different details of *setting* and *aesthetic*, whereas the story is almost always about *people and their actions*.

There are, of course, always exceptions. Some stories return to exactly the same balance of forces as when they started; some end with a deliberate lack of resolution in order to unsettle or disturb; while some employ the use of a deus ex machina: the heroes, seemingly defeated, are saved at the very last moment with the arrival of reinforcements (e.g. Fortinbras turns up at the end of *Hamlet* to restore order).

Five-act Structure

Shakespeare's plays are written in five acts, with the tragedies broken down, according to scholar A. C. Bradley, as follows:

- *Act One* – Exposition
- *Act Two* – Development
- *Act Three* – Crisis
- *Act Four* – Denouement
- *Act Five* – Catastrophe/Resolution

When telling a story in three scenes you may find that you are jumping to the main sections in order to get to the heart of the drama. You might skip over some of the early developments in order to get to the crisis, and skip later developments in order to reach the resolution. In effect, you are truncating – skipping Acts Two and Four, or squeezing elements of those acts into the other three.

There are obvious differences with five-scene stories, not least greater room for development and consequence.

With five scenes instead of three, the story is likely to be longer. This isn't a rule – you could tell a five-scene story in five minutes and a three-scene story in half an hour, but for now let's assume that the extra two chapters will add length to the narrative.

Macbeth

Act One (Exposition)

- The witches deliver their prophecy to Macbeth and Banquo.

- Macbeth is promoted to Thane of Cawdor.

- Duncan announces Malcolm as his successor and Macbeth realises that Malcolm now stands between him and the throne.

- Lady Macbeth attempts to persuade her husband that he must kill Duncan.

- Duncan arrives at Macbeth's castle as an honoured guest.

- Macbeth tells Lady Macbeth that he is unable to kill the king.

Act Two (Development)

- Macbeth kills Duncan.
- The murder is revealed but suspicion falls on Malcolm and Donalbain – Duncan's sons – who have fled in fear.

Act Three (Crisis)

- Macbeth, unable to find contentment as King, hires killers to murder Banquo and Fleance.
- Banquo is murdered but Fleance escapes.
- Macbeth sees Banquo's ghost at a banquet and those around Macbeth believe him to be losing his mind.

Act Four (Denouement)

- Macbeth consults the witches who tell him 'none of woman born shall harm Macbeth' and that he will never be vanquished 'until Birnham Wood comes to Dunsinane'.
- On hearing that Macduff has fled to England and that forces are conspiring against him, Macbeth has Macduff's family killed.
- Macduff, in England, hears news of his family's death and, allied with Malcolm, swears revenge.

Act Five (Catastrophe/Resolution)

- Lady Macbeth, sleepwalking, talks of Duncan's murder.
- Forces rallying against Macbeth use the cover of branches from Birnham Wood and advance on the tyrant.
- Lady Macbeth dies.

- It appears as if the wood is advancing on Dunsinane.
- Macduff (born by caesarean) confronts and defeats Macbeth.
- Order is restored and Malcolm is to be crowned King.

Another example

Remember our story about Chandra and Max? How might that, break down into five scenes instead of just three? (Notice that as this is not classical tragedy, the chapters now have different headings.)

Scene One (Exposition and 'The Premise')

- Chandra and Max prepare for their party.
- Max is hopeful of meeting someone but anxious about their new house getting trashed.
- Chandra reminds him that 'fortune favours the brave' and he will have to take a risk if he wants a reward.
- Max asks Chandra if she is worried about her possessions being damaged. Chandra shrugs it all off. She's had a miserable few months and wants to let her hair down and party.
- Max suggests cancelling the party but the doorbell rings. It's too late.

Scene Two (Catalyst and Development)

- The party begins and all goes well to start with.
- Max is propelled into the party when Annika asks him to dance, and they get on well.

- Chandra gets drunk.
- The party starts to spin out of control.

Scene Three (High Point or Crisis)

- Chandra hides in Max's bedroom and tries to persuade him to call off the party.
- Max resists, excited that things are going well with Annika.
- Chandra decides to call the police and report their overenthusiastic guests. Max is angry with her for this.

Scene Four (Low Point)

- The police arrive and break up the party.
- Chandra sees that some of her possessions are broken.
- Max realises that Annika has gone and wishes he had never listened to Chandra.

Scene Five (Resolution)

- Max finds a note from Annika, pinned to Chandra's piano, leaving her phone number, and decides the risk was worth taking after all.

Those five chapters have now become:

- Exposition and premise.
- Catalyst and development.
- High point or crisis.
- Low point.
- Resolution.

Five Chapters in Any Sequence

Just as we played *Three Chapters in Any Sequence* (page 178), we can now do the same with five beats of a story.

While working on *Showstopper!* we often feel our way through a show in five sections, similar to the five-act breakdown of Shakespeare's tragedies (pages 182–5):

1. A platform and premise.

2. Catalyst and development.

3. High point, crisis, or cliffhanger.

4. Low point.

5. Resolution.

We can also feel our way through a show in three broader sections:

1. Premise.

2. Development.

3. Resolution.

It doesn't matter if we are telling a classic 'hero story', a tragedy, an epic or a romantic comedy – these shapes always make for a more satisfying journey. Sometimes we come off stage and feel there was something missing from the story we had just told. Because we film every show, we can watch them back to find out what happened. Usually we identify the lack of a satisfying low or high point, or notice that a low point had been negated (a problem had been solved too quickly) or wasn't given enough time to breathe.

During the show performers who are observing the action from offstage never discuss story beats, arcs or choices. In fact, we never discuss anything at all. Not least because talking to each other distracts us from what is happening on stage.

Instead, we try to play with our favourite maxim: 'If it's good, make it better; if it's bad, make it worse,' which means that, in performance, the whole team is pulling in the same direction. It stops us from negating story arcs and helps us to give the story a full dynamic range of peaks and troughs.

High points and low points – a sense of shape

A story needs a sense of shape. A simple way of approaching this is to consider a high point and a low point.

Macbeth, it could be argued, is at his highest point in Act Two, when he realises he will be King, the natural zenith of his ambition as prophesied by the witches. His lowest point might be in Act Five, when he hears his wife is dead and that Birnham Wood is marching on Dunsinane. Another significant low point occurs earlier in Act Three, when he sees the ghost of Banquo and realises he is too deeply saturated in horrific crimes ever to be truly free again.

In our story about Max and Chandra (pages 175–7), Max reaches his high point when he thinks something romantic is going to happen with Annika, and his low point when he sees she has been scared off by the arrival of the police, leaving him with nothing but mess and despair.

In Anya and Tony's wedding (pages 179–81), the wedding itself is the high point.

In classical tragedy, the lowest moment is when the protagonist realises they are the cause of their own misfortune. Oedipus, realising he has killed his father, married his mother, and brought wrath to Thebes, plucks out his own eyes. Safe to consider this a low moment, I think.

The hero, at their lowest moment, should be lower than we have seen them at any other point in the narrative thus far. They must be worse off than when they started.

There will be a series of peaks and troughs for most of the characters – certainly the protagonist(s) – but knowing that one peak will be the highest and one trough will be the lowest helps a company give its story shape.

To find these high points and low points the company must be aware of where they are in the running time of the presentation. If you are performing a one-hour story, the lowest moment is likely to come somewhere towards the end, ideally with enough time to move into a fifth and final act, or at least the conclusion of the story. There might be a turnaround, a twist of fate or a tragic ending, but there needs to be enough time remaining for any of these options to breathe. Nor can the low point come too early. If it happens after fifteen minutes there will be difficulties sustaining a bridge, lasting forty-five minutes, to the end. It is more likely that the company will have to find another, even lower moment, towards the end. Martin Scorsese's film *After Hours* features a series of disasters for Griffin Dunne as he desperately tries to get home. Things get worse and worse for our protagonist, until eventually the sun comes up and he has to go straight back into work and start his day all over again (the final frames being a reincorporation of the first).

More Than Five Chapters

Once players are practised at three- and five-scene stories, you can open it up into any number of scenes. A story in seven scenes? A story in fifteen scenes in any sequence? The principles are the same. You could play this for years and never tire of the options and possibilities.

Practising with a pre-set number of scenes (both in and out of sequence) helps the player to make decisions accordingly. Players starting with the final scene of a seven-scene story are looking for resolution and harmony rather than argument and discord. Players who jump into the middle of a story should explore events of real significance, as this is likely to be the heart of the drama.

Even a story told out of sequence settles into the feel of a Beginning – Middle – End story, because that's how the audience experiences it. Dramatists and filmmakers who play fast and loose with structure will still find that an audience responds to whatever they see first as the start of their engagement with the story, its world and characters, and whatever happens next to be the middle, and the last stages inevitably the end.

The classic longform Harold plays in three sets of three scenes (Beginning – Middle – End). Regardless of what structure your longform takes, you could look at the story you have told afterwards and retrospectively divide it into these sections.

No matter how many acts, chapters or beats your story is told in, it is likely to have the same shape of any single scene – exposition (set-up), development of premise and resolution.

Status Quo and Catalyst

The animation masters Pixar have a formula they put to writers which goes something like this:

>Once upon a time in the land of ___.

>There was a ___.

>Every day they ___.

>Until one day ___ happened.

>Which led to ___.

>Which led to ___.

>Which led to ___.

…And so on.

Another way to explore the ideas of premise, status quo and catalyst (or inciting incident) is a game I credit to fellow Showstopper and teacher Sean McCann.

Movie Trailers

This is essentially a variant on the old 'typewriter' game in which one person narrates and the others play out characters in the story, the action switching between the two.

The first, in the style of Don LaFontaine, the famously deep gravelly voice-over artist for movie trailers:

In a world where ___, one woman decided to ___.

The second played as a romcom or 'wacky comedy' trailer:

___ was just an ordinary guy – until one day ___.

Have one person provide the voice-over and intercut it with a group of players presenting short extracts from the film. The whole exercise need not last longer than two minutes. It's good practice for quick platform-builds and discovery of the premise. Use music that suits the exercise.

Having improvised a narrative, look back over your show and briefly summarise the story as if it were a movie trailer. If it seems to work in this context your story probably had a satisfying shape to it.

What World is This?

Before the status quo changes, or a character is propelled on an adventure, it is necessary to know a little about the story's setting, especially its *mood* and *values*.

Macbeth begins with a storm upon 'a blasted heath'. Nature and society are being torn apart by the chaos of war and supernatural forces.

Legally Blonde opens in sunny Los Angeles, where appearance, gossip, friendship and romance are the strongest forces in the life of the heroine Elle.

The first scenes of the narrative will establish this tone. Who are the people in this world, and what is their day-to-day routine? Improvisers will use the skills of joining and pattern recognition to discover this early on.

For example: A story begins with two characters in a trendy restaurant. They are both relaxed, happy. Nothing important appears to be at stake. They are talking about the publication of a book. We learn that one character is an author, the other their publisher. As the publisher starts to field numerous phone calls and their conversation is interrupted by drop-in characters vying for the publisher's attention (initially one player and then others, building on the original offer to create a pattern), we realise we are in the world of 'busy artistic and successful professionals' – a world the author longs to aspire to. We might discover something of the moral value of this world too: 'You have to be in with the right crowd to get ahead in this game' or 'What will it take to get noticed in a world saturated with content?'

Or: Two knights are soon to leave Camelot to go on a quest. Camelot represents safety, security, and honest, decent people. The first knight prays, revealing some pious characteristics. The second player, joining in prayer, competes to be holier and worthier. A pattern emerges in which we learn about the moral values of the knights as well as their rivalry.

The *broadening* skill, with numerous separate ideas being introduced, is useful when building platforms for scenes in the foundation of a story. The play *Macbeth* does not solely establish conflict, furthering that one idea at the expense of others; it also explores a friendship between Macbeth and Banquo, a loyalty in their service to the King, and supernatural elements in the form of the witches. A status quo is likely to have numerous elements to it. Themes in our 'Camelot' story include holiness and worship, danger outside the city, and a certain rivalry between our heroes.

Some guidelines for playing story games and exercises

In shortform improv, the players, within normal social confines of taste and appropriateness, are pretty much free to act on any impulse as soon as they experience it. As the games and scenes don't need to connect, the consequences of a player's actions end with the scene or game.

In longform and narrative improv, however, choices made at any given moment might affect the entire story. Consequently, players' impulses are channelled through the lens of the overall narrative, ensuring that most ideas are kept within the circle of expectation.

If the first half-hour of a show has been a naturalistic, domestic family drama with gentle development of light-hearted relationships and emotions, a sudden lurch to dark or murderous deeds will likely feel like a jolt. Not to say this can't happen, of course. *The Deer Hunter* famously spends almost a glacially paced hour showing the interaction of Pennsylvania steelworkers and their families before a sudden jump takes us to the intense horrors of the Vietnam War. The abrupt and shocking change is effective. Improvising such wild turns is possible, but players would be encouraged to practise building within the circle of ideas until they have more experience and familiarity with one another.

Remember – draw like da Vinci before you paint like Picasso.

Fears and concerns experienced by players within a scene are magnified in the context of the story as a whole. Try to keep ideas connected. Focus on relationships and interaction (regardless of genre, which can often be regarded as decorative in improv), and move one beat at a time.

If you have a thrilling idea for where the story might go, consider the following:

- You can only make one offer at a time. If players build on your offer as you expected, fine. If not, yield and change.

- Even if your idea doesn't get picked up by your fellow players as you expected, it could develop into something more wonderful than you imagined.

- If you really can't let go of those ideas, be a writer instead. Improvised narrative work is a team game and, although it is possible to tilt the sail or nudge the rudder, you cannot dominate control of the boat without risking tyranny or mutiny.

So is there still really no such thing as a mistake?

Embracing apparent mistakes works excellently in shortform improv where an entire scene can quite happily grow from one. In longform, however, everything that happens relates to a single narrative. With scenes connected according to the principles of dramatic structure, some decisions could lead us away from a satisfying through-line. Decisions are no longer purely ephemeral – they might impact the whole story and have longer-lasting consequences.

Here is an example:

In the first scene of a ninety-minute improvised narrative, Louise, a barista in a local coffee shop, has fallen in love/lust with a regular customer called Miguel. We know this because we have been watching Louise with her friend and co-worker Emily, and they have been talking about it. Louise would love to ask Miguel out, but she lacks the confidence to do so.

Yes, there is no such thing as a mistake and, yes, players can work with any ideas – *but some decisions now would clearly be better than others.*

If Miguel were to enter and ask Louise out, then it negates many of the offers that have already been made and accepted. In this scenario the players have discovered a tension (unrequited attraction), which could serve as a premise for the unfolding drama, were it not immediately negated ('It's okay – I want to go out with you anyway!'). Of course, the story *can* continue. This offer doesn't *destroy* the narrative, but it does weaken it by negating much of what we have already established. The audience will eventually tire of too many negations. It's like having a conversation with someone who constantly changes their mind. It can be infuriating.

If Louise suddenly decides to leave town and move to another country, we can happily follow her and the story, but we would probably be left thinking: 'Why all that talk about Miguel at the start?' The players would need to reincorporate Miguel later in the narrative (or at least the significance of Louise's attraction to him) for the story to be completely satisfying.

Mistakes start to feel like mistakes in longform/narrative improv when they oppose the natural flow of scenic connection or when they are ignored and abandoned. The unrelated tends to stand out.

So just as you would find when writing a story, some decisions are better than others. The spontaneity of improvising this process, with no option to rewrite or revise, gives performer and audience an added frisson of danger.

A story can sustain any choice made by any player. The question is, how much time do you have to explore the consequences of those choices? If you are in the last five minutes of your show you simply do not have time to open up a whole new idea and explore it to any satisfying degree. Towards the end of any story reincorporation is the most effective technique. The further you move outside the circle of expected ideas the longer it will take you to complete your story and return to what the audience expects.

It is also wise to ask yourself at all times: 'Where is the focus?' and 'Whose scene is this?' Addressing questions like these will mean players are more sensitive to supporting characters, to the timing of entering and exiting, to understanding the scene and dramatic development, and staging choices.

For example, in the story of Louise and Miguel, Louise is the focus of Scene One. Her needs and desires are the dramatic impetus of the scene. The actor playing Emily would notice this as the scene unfolds and therefore serve as sidekick/friend/adviser to Louise. Other characters could drop in and out of the scene but should realise that the scene is not about them.

But what if...?

But what if someone came into the Louise/Emily scene and created a new story about something completely different?

As in the scene-building game *'What Happens Next?'* (page 66), a single idea is furthered until such a point as a second idea emerges, either by design or by accident. Reaching this point means there are now two story strands to work with.

In rehearsals you can stop and analyse why a decision is being made and what its consequences might be. In performance, you work with what is. If a new story has been added, try to find the relationship between the two stories. Why are both of these story strands important?

Different genres require different techniques and approaches. Satisfying sleuth stories need twists. A futuristic spy thriller might have complex plotting, whereas a family drama may have gentler dramatic movement based upon relationships. The storytelling processes remain the same but the aesthetic changes according to genre.

◊ ◊ ◊

Tragedy v. Comedy

These giants of form have countless books and essays dedicated to them, but it is worth outlining them here briefly before we move on.

Tragedy

Aristotle defined tragedy as a form which brings about *catharsis* – a purging of fear and pity – in the spectators.

In classical tragedy the tragic hero has a *harmatia* or tragic flaw, which is the cause of their downfall and which they do not recognise in themselves until it is too late – a moment of *anagnorisis*.

It will end with the protagonist's death (and other characters may suffer and die along the way).

In improvising a tragedy it would be good to establish the protagonist's flaw early on (Macbeth's is ambition, Othello's is jealousy).

In early experiments with my Shakespearean improv troupe The School of Night we would improvise classical tragedies, asking the audience to provide the tragic hero's flaw.

Comedy

Tales of miscommunication, misunderstandings and mistakes, which end in harmony – often a wedding or union. Order is eventually restored, although what the characters have learned varies from comedy to comedy.

When improvising in comedy form, push the misunderstandings as far as they can go, then look to find understanding, harmony and resolution in the closing act.

Examples from Showstopper! *of a tragedy and a comedy*

I remember two different *Showstopper!* stories, each beginning with the same premise. While one developed into a comedy, the other became a tragedy.

A young knight is in love with a noblewoman and arrives at court to woo her.

In the comedy, the knight's rebuttal after his early attempts at courtship lead him to re-enter the noblewoman's court, disguised as a woman. The noblewoman, enamoured with the knight but keen to test his character, eventually sees through his deception and disguises herself as a knight, resulting in playful explorations of love and gender. The story ends harmoniously when all confusions are revealed and disguises unveiled.

In the tragic version, the knight is unable to recognise the difference between objects of affection and his objectification of women. Ignoring the warnings and refusing to relinquish his desires, he kills his rival suitors until he too is eventually slain by the noblewoman.

You might quite reasonably ask: how I am supposed to be in the moment while maintaining an awareness of the whole shape of a story with all its requirements and possibilities? How can I play in the present *and* the future at the same time? Consider that actors in scripted performance work with the past, the present *and* the future. They are aware of their character's 'given circumstances' (past); they focus on their targets and play actions in order to be in the moment (present), and all the while they are in pursuit of an intention (future).

The intention for the actor working with a script is much like the story arc for the narrative improviser. Improvisers do not know what the conclusion of any story arc will be, but they play the moment, discovering how each moment relates to the next and further contextualises the story as a whole. Just as a scene takes shape through connected offers, story takes shape through connected scenes.

One Section at a Time

An effective practice is to have a separate director observing, calling units of action as and when they are required. For example:

- *Scene One* – Establish a status quo, the routine for our characters and some basic information about them. Who is the main character or characters?

- *Scene Two* – Let's meet some other characters who relate to the ones we have already seen.

- *Scene Three* – Some kind of catalyst will occur in the next five minutes that will change things for our main character(s).

- *Scene Four* – Start to explore what happens as a result of these changes.

- *Scene Five* – Everything goes well. Reach a high point.

- *Scene Six* – Everything starts to go badly.

- *Scene Seven* – Make it worse. Drive the hero to their low point!

- *Scene Eight* – Start to reincorporate to find a way out of this trouble.

- *Scene Nine* – Resolve, reincorporate, find harmony.

Here, in nine scenes, should be a whole narrative with a sense of shape and clarity. Some longforms play with a fixed number of scenes. You can have any number of scenes in narrative improvisations.

Try some variations:

Scene lengths

Not all scenes are the same length. For those of you who play shortform improv you will notice that many games have patterns which, once established, speed up. There will be times in the narrative when shorter scenes are desirable.

Play a five-scene story with set times on each chapter of the story, e.g:

- *Chapter One* = 4 minutes
- *Chapter Two* = 3.5 minutes
- *Chapter Three* = 5 minutes
- *Chapter Four* = 2.5 minutes
- *Chapter Five* = 2 minutes

Or more ambitiously, play out of sequence, as follows:

- *Chapter Four* = 3 minutes
- *Chapter One* = 1.5 minutes
- *Chapter Five* = 2 minutes
- *Chapter Three* = 7 minutes
- *Chapter Two* = 4 minutes

In *Showstopper!* practice sessions I test the company by giving them a fixed time in which to play an entire musical: 'This musical is forty-five minutes long' or 'Nineteen-and-a-half minutes exactly.' The players synchronise watches and shape their story as they play, depending on where they are on the clock. The team develops a collective feel for when to speed up, slow down, let things breathe, or move things on. Players often pull in different directions and have to learn when to yield. There is a thrilling sense of achievement when the last note of the final song ends precisely on the final second of the allocated time.

Note that playing with these restrictions will most likely cause tension for some performers, but working with tension, and learning how to reduce it or thrive with it, is excellent practice for improvisers.

Starting in the middle

As you connect scenes into an overall narrative and the story gathers momentum, you will find that not every scene need start with an expositional platform. Once we get to know characters and their environments, scenes can begin in the middle of the action. Another old maxim challenges writers to be 'the last one in and the first one out', to encourage economy in scenic construction. Try starting your first offer with the word 'and' – a simple trick that forces you to be in some kind of ongoing action.

Editing

Many longforms employ a 'sweep edit', which is where one performer moves in a line downstage of the action, as if to sweep the scene away and initiate a new one. Any player can do this at any time, which tests improvisers' sensitivities to scene and story. If you are part of a group you can develop your own ways to initiate edits and scene endings. If you have the good fortune to work with a skilled lighting improviser, they can 'edit' scenes for you.

Montages

A montage sequence uses short fragments of scenes to condense the passing of time. It is a particularly popular device in movies.

In the 1980s TV show *The A-Team* each episode would see the A-Team, deep in trouble, have to build some kind of weapon or machine to get themselves out of danger and save the day. Cue music and a montage. The *Rocky* films made the 'training montage' something of a movie staple. In Trey Parker and Matt Stone's *Team America* the team famously sing 'We're gonna need a montage' in a sequence that condenses the passage of time.

Montages are used to span time and/or traverse geographical distances. The opening ten minutes of Pixar's film *Up* is a montage prologue spanning almost sixty years in the life of a couple before the real narrative begins.

Here's an example of how montages might be staged in improvisation:

We begin with a single hero learning martial arts.

This montage sequence will consist of *three rounds* with *three interactions* in each round.

1. Three separate offers are made, inspired by the idea of martial arts', e.g. a Jackie Chan–style attack move, a somersault, trying to catch a bird, breaking a brick with a single blow. Our hero is incompetent in each instance (for they are at the beginning of their journey).

2. The same three offers are made again to our hero but now she has gained a certain degree of competence. Time has passed and she has improved.

3. Finally, the same three offers are made again, and our hero surpasses herself, not just with competence but with mastery.

Musical underscoring is highly recommended!

The *Showstopper!* company often rehearsed a new technique by working to an exact preset structure like the one above. We would create a pattern and practise it diligently. We would then create a completely different pattern and practise that, and so on with numerous patterns until eventually we abandoned all patterns and structures, playing according to storytelling principles and our experience. It was no longer important that we specifically played three rounds of three scenes. All that mattered was the potential for discovery of new patterns in the moment to clearly communicate progress and compression of time. In one show, for example, the company showed a character's gradual mastery of opera during fifteen short exchanges.

We played training montages, passage-of-time montages, and indeed told whole life stories in montage form.

Develop your own blueprints for montages. Develop as many as you can. And then forget about the exact shapes, trusting that you will have retained the principles, which essentially are as follows:

- Play episodically, in short exchanges and fragments (a single offer and response can be an effective unit of action).

- Make significant change over the duration of the sequence.

- Aim for shorter exchanges and interactions.

- Reincorporating offers demonstrates that time has passed.

- Maintain a sense of momentum. Scenes should get shorter or speed up rather than get longer and slow down.

There are many kinds of montages, and each group will experiment and find different games and frameworks that work best for them. Here are a few ideas to get you started:

A travel montage where a character or characters go on a long journey:

- A hot-air-balloon race around the world.

- A road trip across America.

- A cruise ship around the Bahamas.

A training montage where a character or characters:

- Go from the lowest rung of the ladder in a business and work their way up, eventually becoming the boss.

- Achieve mastery in a skill they previously knew nothing about (archery, tightrope-walking, computer hacking).

- Build a bridge or a skyscraper.

Other montages you could try include:

- A passage-of-time sequence from freshers' week at university to graduation day.

- A couple meeting, falling in love, moving through the many stages of a relationship, right through to marriage. (Why stop there? Try that prologue from Pixar's *Up*.)

- Two friends going in very different directions in life over the course of five years, one going up in the world, the other struggling and sinking.

…and remember: If it's good, make it better; if it's bad, make it worse.

Spins

Spins are flashbacks or flash-fowards, movements to another point of time in the story that, once explored, return to the original scene and pick up the action where it left off.

You have probably seen a movie in which someone begins to remember an event that happened years ago. The camera slowly closes in on their face, the image becomes blurry (the most clichéd version involves dreamy harp music), and as clarity of focus is restored, we find ourselves in the very past they were describing.

A spin can be initiated by players at any time in a scene or story if it would be more interesting to watch the anticipated drama unfold rather than have it reported in speech from the present. If a groom remembers how drunk his parents were on the dance floor at his wedding, it might be more enjoyable to watch that dancing happening in a flashback, rather than listening to it being described.

Every player or group can develop their own ways of initiating spins.

The stage picture must, of course, transform so that we are in a recognisably different time and space.

Unless you are playing a series of quickfire gags, coming back to the present at the end of the spin scene must inform the characters in some way – otherwise why spin at all? Why was that story shared? How has the telling of it, and the listening to it, affected and changed the characters on stage?

Single spins with music

Play a scene with two characters. Any kind of scene in any genre, with relationship and setting established in advance or discovered during the scene.

After the first part of the scene (the platform) has been established and the scene is developing, either character can initiate a spin. This could be as simple as: 'Do you remember that time when...?'

Your musician is observing the action and awaiting a cue like this so they can initiate the spin. If you are working without a musician, the audience could prompt the performers into this development by something as simple as calling out 'spin'.

Then play out the new scene. This might be in a different location from the original scene and it might involve other actors. An example might be:

1. A brother and sister are going through their mother's possessions following her death. They find a photograph of themselves as kids.

2. They spin back into a scene when they were kids, play that new scene, and then spin back to the present to complete the original scene.

You might find it useful to endow the memory with a few details so that you have starting points for what you explore in flashback. For example, the brother and sister, on finding the photograph, might say:

   — Yes, I remember – it was Christmas Eve and we
     were up late in our room, too excited to sleep and
     talking about Christmas...

Or:

   — Look, this is us with Sanjay. Remember he used to
     live next door but came over to our house all the
     time because he was obsessed with your computer
     games?

Music and lighting can be used to move in and out of the spin and give it a feel/tone or mood different from the main scene.

A flash-forward can also be played.

- — Imagine what life will be like when we finally have our own house. I can see it now. Kids running around, friends and neighbours over in the garden, a summer barbecue…

Or:

- — When I grow up I am going to be an explorer. I can picture myself now, leading an expedition through the Amazon…

Sex and the City

This is a game I developed while at LAMDA and one that always proved enjoyable to play and entertaining to watch.

The popular television show *Sex and the City* featured four women with contrasting characteristics, meeting regularly for lunch and often sharing stories about their recent sexual encounters. The men in these encounters were known by nicknames such as 'Jazz Man' or 'Comic Book Guy'. In this game you can play with gender fluidity as you wish – and it doesn't have to be limited to heterosexual relationships.

We begin with four women at lunch and establish a platform, by players endowing each other to discover their status differences and most defining characteristics.

There could be a waiter or other drop-ins to help facilitate the scene.

After a while any of the characters can say to another:

- A. How did your date go the other night with – [*Insert nickname, e.g. Wolf Boy or Aztec Man*]?

- B. Yes, tell us all about it, didn't you go to the – [*Insert location for date/meeting, e.g. the funfair, the bowling alley, that fancy new restaurant, an immersive theatre experience*]?

To which the actor can reply:

    C. Well, it was very – [*Insert one descriptive word to give a feel for how the evening went, e.g. strange, hilarious, intense, passionate.*]

Having endowed a characteristic for the date, a location for the event, and a tone for the scene, the players all spin and play out the date, spinning back to the four ladies lunching when the scene is over.

Each spin story somehow affects the four characters when we return to them in the present. Over time, all four characters have their spins so that we see all four dates played out.

    A. Hey, didn't you go out with Jalapeño Joe last night?

    B. Oh, that's right, I hear he took you to a baseball game!

    C. Yes, he did, but you know what – it turned out to be one of the most romantic evenings of my life!

    [*And spin...*]

A typical game lasts twenty or thirty minutes and there is always room for additions and variations. The whole game can be played with four actors doubling and playing all the dates and other characters throughout, or played with a large group, so other performers drop in and out of each spin. Often we wanted to see the date go further so additional spins were added ('And then you went back to his place, didn't you? What was that like? What happened?').

The game can be played with four men, or a mix of men and women, and you can explore any kind of relationship you wish.

As with *Emotional Taxi* (page 123), find a way of completing the scene once all the games have been played and all the spins have been seen. Reincorporate to finish.

I have also played this game with music – both as underscoring, and to allow performers to sing songs at any time.

Sometimes the scenes find some kind of narrative connection, but there is no pressure to do so. The game is fundamentally about endowment and spins.

Story Jump

A five-player game.

Player A begins a solo scene. Remember to engage with activity and emotion.

As in *Quartets* (page 116), allow the scene to develop and get the second player to identify a beat-change before entering.

Both A and B now jump to a brand-new scene – new setting, new characters, new content.

After a while, a third player enters. Now A, B and C all jump to a new scene. And so on, until the fifth player enters, at which point all five players play a one-minute scene.

After this, character E exits and the four remaining players jump back to complete their four-person story. Character D exits, leaving A, B and C to complete their three-person scene, and so on until A is left alone and must complete their opening solo scene.

The most important part of this exercise is to make a time-jump every time a player exits. Players should skip over the middle part of the scene and jump to the ending, rather than continuing the scene from where they left off.

Encourage players to use whatever physical position they are in when the scene jumps and continue from that point, rather than correcting their physicality and resetting to a neutral posture. This position is an opening offer, not something to be ignored, and can therefore help players make the jump. (A lot like the well-known improv game 'Freeze Tag', in which an observer pauses the action by calling 'Freeze!' replaces one of the players, taking up their exact physical position, and then begins a new scene from that position.)

Things to look out for

While improvisers are trained to respond immediately to their instincts, it might not always be suitable in this game. Entering and changing the scene before it has had any time to establish itself will not only feel unsettling but will make it difficult to return to. This is one of the big differences between shortform and longform playing. Storytelling requires performers to match their instincts against the developing story. Not every *personal* impulse will be helpful to the *communal* story.

Backwards

Harold Pinter's play *Betrayal* and Stephen Sondheim and George Furth's musical *Merrily We Roll Along* are both narratives explored in reverse.

Play a scene starting with the last line or final beat, then work backwards one offer at a time until you are at the start. A good way of exploring this is with an interview (this idea courtesy of improviser Inbal Lori).

Set up an interviewer and guest, and maybe a reason for the discussion – promotion of an academic's new book or actor's new film, for example. Don't worry if this pushes you into a thinking space. It's a challenging exercise so it may well cause some strain. As always with such challenges break it down into smaller chunks. Look at what has just happened and ask yourself what might have happened immediately before to create this beat. Keep moving one beat backwards and don't try to control the whole story or scene. It's also a good exercise in encouraging big, bold decisions, and reminding players to play fast, contrasting actions.

You may have already done something like this in *Three Chapters in Any Sequence* (page 178). If not, return to that exercise and play:

1. End

2. Middle

3. Beginning

Observe what happens in the End scene and plant the seeds for it when you finally get to the Beginning scene.

Other Story Forms

This would be a good time to return to *Quartets* (page 116). Originally played as an exercise in scene-building and development, it's now approached as a way of exploring an entire story within a single scene – platform, catalyst, crisis, resolution – all in linear time with no jumps or edits.

Revolving Doors

A game best suited to a larger group of around ten players, although if you have time it will sustain more.

Agree upon a setting, something where characters who know each other can gather – a wedding, a funeral, a school reunion, etc.

Begin with two players and allow them to build a platform and develop a scene. From this point on any new character can enter, but when they do so one of the previous players must exit (one in, one out, as if through a metaphorical revolving door).

Players can return at any time as the same character or a different one.

This game is all about making connections and will help to show how a story can still be satisfying simply as a series of connected characters and events.

All these group narrative games help develop sensitivity. Has enough been established in the scene before I enter? Does it matter if I go in early? Which one of us should exit? Has everyone played a scene? The answers to these questions are all entirely situation-dependent and there are no set rules, but we can again remind ourselves of the principles of storytelling. What is this scene about, and what kind of story is unfolding?

I have played variations of this game where, in order to reach a satisfying conclusion, any number of characters can be on stage together by the end.

Chain of Fools

Of all the games and storytelling exercises, this is my favourite. I'd like to see it played more in performance. I'm sure there are all sorts of variations, but here is the version I know.

Five players stand in a line facing the audience: from left to right, A, B, C, D and E.

Each player will play scenes only with the person next to them in the chain.

The game requires a set-up as follows:

- Starting with C and D, agree upon a relationship between the two characters and a starting location, e.g. a married couple in their garden, C the wife and D the husband.

- Then D, the husband, has a relationship and location with E, e.g. the husband's best friend – scenes starting in a bar.

- Then C, the wife, has a relationship and location with B, e.g. the wife's sister – scenes starting on a boating trip.

- And finally B, the sister, has a relationship and location with A, e.g. a psychic whom the wife's sister consults in a caravan in the woods.

Don't take too long over this set-up. Go with the first suggestions if you like them.

So now all five players have a character and a relationship with the person next to them in the chain. They also know where their first scenes are set.

C and D (husband and wife) play a scene in their garden. At any stage, someone from the next link in the chain can tag their partner and the action switches to a new scene with those players. For example: if C and D are playing a scene, E can tag D (now the husband is playing a scene with his best friend in a bar) or B can tag C (and the sister is playing a scene with the wife on a boating trip).

You can only tag the person next to you in the chain, so A cannot play scenes with C, D or E, they can only play with B.

It appears complicated but everyone will soon get the hang of it.

Let every couple establish a scene for a few minutes and then start to move up and down the chain, eventually playing shorter scenes until, by the end of the game, the company is playing five-second scenes.

Start your first scene in the location you have been given but after this scenes can take place anywhere (so long as you endow the space) and can also happen anywhere in the timeline. The story can run in linear or non-linear time.

Things to look out for

Players won't have to think about a three- or five-act structure here, they are simply looking to find connections and put heat under whatever seems to be happening. The acceleration of the game will give it a sense of structure. You can end however you wish – after a fixed number of scenes or, more usefully, when the group collectively feels it has come to the end.

Players on the ends of the chain will have fewer scenes, but this doesn't mean they can't influence the action. In fact, it is rare that scenes do *not* affect each other. The stories of everyone in the chain almost always become intertwined.

Other examples

- A = B's Blackjack dealer. A and B play their scene at the casino.
- B = C's dangerous best friend. B and C on a transatlantic flight.
- C = D's daughter. C and D at an ice-skating rink.
- D = C's father. D with E at a counselling session.
- E = D's counsellor.

Or:

- A = A science-fiction writer. A and B in a secluded cabin in the country.

- B = A's brother, married to C. B and C are backstage before a big presentation.

- C = A leading scientist. C and D in a cutting-edge research lab.

- D = C's assistant. D meets E while jogging in the park.

- E = A version of D from twenty years in the future.

Storyline

A simple game for getting people to think about what comes before, what comes after, and what's missing. Best played with a minimum of six players, but can sustain up to twenty if you have time.

One player stands extreme stage-right and gives the opening line of a story.

- Once upon a time there was a little girl who had a furious temper.

Another player then stands extreme stage-left and gives the closing line of a very different story.

- …and with that the Alpine forests were never the same again.

From now on, players can stand anywhere in the line between the start and the finish and add another line – another beat of the story. The team must collectively make a story that makes sense and has a satisfying premise, development and reincorporation, but as with so many of these games, players can only contribute a single offer at a time.

After each new player joins the line and makes their offer they all repeat their offers in sequence, moving from stage-right to stage-left, so as to remind everyone of the beats and how the story is taking shape.

Encourage players not to think too long over this one. Try something quickly. If it doesn't work you can simply start again. Play repeatedly and quickly.

Slice of Life

An exercise that lends itself excellently to non-comedic improvisation.

Select one player to be the central character. *Slice of Life* will explore key moments from their entire life story in a series of scenes played out in a non-linear chronology. Traditionally it is played a little like *Revolving Doors* (page 210), in that scenes tend to be with two players only – the protagonist and a new character – although when the new character leaves, the protagonist will always stay on stage and will be in every scene.

Other players will make offers to jump the protagonist to different moments of their life – marriage, birth, death, schooldays, first jobs, first kiss, separation, sibling rivalry, anything you like – although it's important to play it out of sequence.

The first four or five scenes will be seemingly disconnected (broadening), allowing the rest of the time to make connections and join the dots.

The average game lasts around fifty minutes. In *Showstopper!* rehearsals we have played it with drop-ins, extras, choruses and music.

Character in Narrative Improvisation

Wants and intentions

In traditional text-based acting, actors are encouraged to find and understand their characters' intentions or objectives, i.e. What do they want? What drives them?

Time can be spent in the rehearsal room trying to clarify and be specific about intention, but there is no time for this kind of preparation or negotiation in improvised theatre. It's possible to set yourself a want or an intention before you go into a scene, but this can only be a starting point – and one that may limit you. It's also possible to discover what your character wants during a scene or learn what they wanted by the end of a scene.

For example: Macbeth doesn't start out wanting to murder Duncan or to be King. It's only when the witches tell him that he might be King, and when his wife encourages him in this regard, that he begins to consider the options.

Elle doesn't start out wanting to be a Harvard-trained lawyer. To begin with she wants to pick out the perfect dress for what she thinks will be her engagement dinner. She discovers her true desires and potential as the story develops.

In both *Macbeth* and *Legally Blonde* characters' intentions have been predetermined by the writers and form the basic machinations of the story.

In improvisation, exploring the story from within, beat by beat, will often *reveal* intentions.

So in our earlier scene (pages 175–7), for example: the actor playing Max *discovers in Scene One* that he wishes to fall in love and that his fear of damaging the house in a party is an obstacle to his intention.

The actor playing Chandra, by deciding to play an opposing point of view to Max, *discovers* that she wants a party and won't let Max's anxiety get in her way. She discovers that her first intention is to persuade Max that everything will be okay and to stop him from cancelling the party. Later in the story, when she realises she has made a mistake and the party is getting out of hand, she discovers a new intention – to call the police and stop the party herself.

Archetypes

The archetypal characters of *Commedia dell'Arte* have been famously preserved in masks, pictures and a handful of teachers throughout the centuries. The old miser, the fraudulent doctor, the flashy braggart, the sly servant – many of society's well-recognised types frequently appear in these stories. In tales across all cultures throughout the ages we see similar archetypes, suggesting a universality of human experience.

Protagonist

From the Greek 'agon' meaning struggle, i.e. 'the one who undergoes the struggle.' This is why it's essential, when improvising a story with a clear protagonist, to put them through the mincer (dramatically or humorously). I have seen many shows in which the actor improvising the protagonist is too glib to be affected very much, while a different actor playing another character starts to become 'protagonised', because their greater emotional engagement with the story steadily makes them more interesting and sympathetic.

If the protagonist does not go on some kind of journey – be it emotional, spiritual, physical or psychological (ideally, all of these) – the story will feel unsatisfying.

There are many characters in the original *Star Wars* trilogy, but Luke Skywalker is the protagonist. The primary drive of the story, and the biggest struggle, is Luke's.

Protagonists are often driven by selfish wants and desires, eventually relinquished for a greater good.

Active and passive protagonists

An active protagonist who makes decisions, with good or bad consequences, is more dynamic than a passive one, who only reacts to circumstance. Experiment with playing both.

A protagonist can be any kind of character of any status. The film *Trading Places* takes two protagonists in Dan Ackroyd (a wealthy capitalist socialite) and Eddie Murphy (a down-and-out), and follows their journeys as they switch status positions. Willy Russell's musical *Blood Brothers* tells a 'nature v. nurture' story of twin boys, separated at birth and given to very different families – one rich, one poor.

In many fairytales the protagonist is presented with few defining characteristics. They are simply a princess, a pauper, a mother or a hunter. This lack of specificity makes it easier for the reader to identify with the protagonist. Protagonists may not always be likeable, but they must have the audience's sympathy/empathy. Without it the audience cannot experience catharsis or ultimately learn about themselves or the human condition.

Tips for playing protagonists

- Let offers affect you.

- Don't be afraid to make decisions – and mistakes.

- Discover something that you want and reasons why you can't initially have it.

- Resist the call to adventure – at first. But eventually you must go on the journey.

- Your want/desire can be selfish and you may learn to give it up for a greater good.

- Make sure you go through the mincer. If your fellow improvisers aren't steering you to important emotional moments, then you will have to assume endowments (page 95) to make certain that your journey has a satisfying struggle.

- The protagonist's struggle must be greater than any other character's.

Multiple/group protagonist stories

Some stories have two protagonists (*Romeo and Juliet*, *Blood Brothers*, *Hansel and Gretel*) and we follow the paths of both, sometimes individually, sometimes together. *Trading Places* puts the protagonists in contrasting trajectories, so that Eddie Murphy is on the rise while Dan Ackroyd is in decline.

It is possible to have a group protagonist story where relatively equal time and weight is given to each character, while they collectively struggle against the forces of antagonism (*The Great Escape*, *Ozark*, and movies featuring teams of heroes, such as *The Avengers* or *The Fantastic Four*).

Antagonist

Antagonists are forces of opposition. In many respects, a story is only as good as its forces of opposition. The stronger the opposition, the greater the struggle becomes for the protagonist.

There may be one primary antagonist who stands in the way of the protagonist's goal or represents the opposite of their moral values and beliefs.

Most superheroes have a primary antagonist, a sworn enemy who stands above all of their other enemies, known as a *nemesis*.

Sherlock Holmes's nemesis is Moriarty. Not only is he as smart and brilliant as Holmes, but he stands in direct opposition to Holmes's function as a character. Holmes is the ultimate detective, Moriarty is a criminal mastermind. Holmes helps people, Moriarty exploits people. But both share many common characteristics too. Both have exceptional powers of deduction, insight, even musicianship. The protagonist and their nemesis often represent different sides of the same coin, which is why many movie depictions of this relationship contain a line which goes something like: 'You know, we are not so very different, you and I...'

Harry Potter and Voldemort. Dorothy and the Wicked Witch. Spiderman and Venom. Bond and Blofeld. Ellen Ripley and 'the Alien'. The hero–nemesis relationship is one of the most enduring in all fiction.

Playing a nemesis or strong antagonist requires an understanding of the characteristics of the protagonist. If our heroine is a competitive dancer, then her nemesis might also be a dancer in the same competition. They might equally be someone who stands opposed to dance. The nemesis may choose to join or contrast the values and occupation of the protagonist, but whatever choices are made they must stand in the way of the needs and wants of the protagonist.

Not all antagonists are evil. Some are simply obstacles or obstructions (often referred to as 'threshold guardians'). A bank clerk, a bouncer, the black knight on the bridge, a traffic warden – all can stand in the way of the hero and their progress, but none of them need be wicked or have any personal agenda against the protagonist. In *After Hours* Griffin Dunne's character meets all sorts of antagonists who obstruct him in his attempts to get home, including a doorman who comes quite literally out of Kafka's *The Trial*.

Tips for playing antagonists

- Try to understand the drives and values of the protagonist. What do they want and what are their values/beliefs?

- You must be an obstacle to what the protagonist wants.

- If you are a primary antagonist or nemesis, then you are the main force of opposition. The protagonist will only be tested as much as you test them. If you are a nemesis, keep challenging your protagonist until you think you have pushed them to the point of no return – and then keep pushing. A few *Showstopper!* shows have been set in the world of superheroes. Those stories were only ever satisfying if a strong villain pushed the hero as close to destruction as possible. Often the performers had no way of knowing how they would come back from this point of no return, trusting fellow players and the power of reincorporation.

- If you are a threshold guardian, your obstruction will be shorter and episodic – a temporary obstacle or resistance. Once the threshold is crossed, the protagonist may well soon encounter another one.

- Remember that antagonists are human too. What has hurt them? What are their weaknesses and vulnerabilities? (Most antagonists do not think of themselves as 'the villain'.)

Sidekicks/helpers

You've seen it a hundred times – the quirky best friend, the loyal retainer, the wingman, the confidante. Protagonists have people in their lives who help them on their journey. Frodo Baggins has Samwise Gamgee (Sam curiously becomes the protagonist by the very end of *The Lord of the Rings*). Dorothy has Toto, and soon gathers the Scarecrow, the Tin Man and the Cowardly Lion to help her along the Yellow Brick Road. Helper characters can fulfil a number of functions. They encourage the protagonist, giving them faith to pursue their goals. They question the protagonist and their choices or thinking. They allow the protagonist to voice their thoughts and feelings so that we too know what is going on in their otherwise private world.

Tips for playing helpers

- Support your protagonist, even if that support means questioning and challenging them. You can have blind faith in them and love for them, or you can confront their logic or motives.

- Travel with them. They will need you to be a confidante and sounding board.

- And remember that just because you are serving the protagonist doesn't mean you can't be an important character in your own right.

Mentors

Albus Dumbledore, Yoda, Gandalf, Mr Miyagi...

The mentor may serve many different functions, including teacher, guide, coach, but fundamentally they are the primary source of *wisdom* for a protagonist. They see the hero's flaws and know what they need to learn to become a better person – usually through insight, but occasionally by accident.

Romeo has Friar Laurence and Juliet has the Nurse (who also acts as her sidekick).

Mentors often give gifts or advice. Bilbo Baggins, mentoring his nephew Frodo, gives him the sword Sting.

There is as much variety in this archetype as in any other – the cool teacher, the 'sink-or-swim' coach, the wounded healer, etc.

There is often a feeling that the mentor has already been a protagonist in their own story in the past (Luke Skywalker is a mentor to Rey in *The Last Jedi*, but he was the protagonist in the original *Star Wars* trilogy), which is often why they have insight and understanding relevant to the hero's condition or situation.

Tips for playing mentors

- Give advice.

- Give gifts.

- Don't overburden the protagonist. A single gift or piece of advice can be enough.

- It can be effective to know the protagonist or one of their relatives ('I was a friend of your father's...').

- Help the protagonist to learn and grow – and understand they may well resist this for a while.

- Again – mentors should be fully realised characters in their own right.

Tricksters

Most mythologies have some kind of trickster – Gollum, Jack Sparrow, Puck... And exactly who is that detective in J. B. Priestley's *An Inspector Calls*...?

It isn't always easy to know whose side a trickster is on. Indeed, they may switch allegiances, follow their own agenda, or have no fixed agenda at all. The trickster can help or hinder, can be useful or dangerous. Sam and Frodo don't know if they can trust Gollum, but they have no choice but to follow him into Mordor.

Tips for playing tricksters

- You don't have to decide on an agenda. Ideally, keep changing your agenda according to what makes it most interesting to the protagonist's journey and the unfolding narrative.

- Don't be afraid to completely change or reverse your point of view.

- Use tricksters sparingly in a narrative. They should tamper joyfully with the fabric of the story, not become the focus of it.

It is often easier to spot these archetypes in genres like fantasy or science-fiction, but they are equally prevalent in domestic and mundane settings. *Whiplash* centres on the relationship between a young jazz drummer and his controversial mentor. *When Harry Met Sally* sees both our eponymous characters teamed up with sidekicks (who are in a relationship with each other).

Shakespeare's plays are filled with servants who act as sidekicks and helpers.

Try creating a story without any of these key archetypes and see what happens.

Macbeth, whose story is largely about subversion of the natural world, is an anti-hero protagonist, with Macduff and Malcolm as antagonists. Macbeth murders his sidekick (Banquo) and mentor (Duncan), as advised by tricksters (the Witches).

Scenes with Archetypes

Play scenes with strong status differences. Then play with archetypes. Start with classic fairytales and fantasy settings, but then take these same relationships into domestic and mundane settings. Try...

Protagonist and mentor

- A drinker and bartender in a downtown bar.
- Someone on a yoga retreat with their guru.

- A stand-up comedian before their first gig and an old-school comic.
- A couple (joint protagonists) and an unorthodox counsellor.
- A parent with their genius child.
- A driving lesson.

Protagonist and antagonist

- Someone trying to get a reservation at an exclusive restaurant.
- A child who wants to get onto the football team, but the school bully is the captain.
- A parent desperate to get help with their online dating profile from their reluctant child.
- Someone applying for a loan at a bank.
- A golfer with an obstructive caddy.

We have mentioned some of the difficulties with *resistance* – where the improviser is unwilling to follow instruction or invitation – and in most cases a scene should move forward in spite of resistance. Here, however, unless the antagonist creates obstacles in some form, then they are probably not serving their function as antagonist.

Protagonist and trickster

- A homeowner hires an unusual and eccentric new gardener.
- A police officer is called to the house of someone who claims to be the victim of a burglary, but all is not as it seems...
- A budding rap star being interviewed by someone claiming to be very important in the music industry.

- A spy receiving secret instructions from a new contact.
- A child asking their sibling to cover for them so they can go out without their parents' permission.

Protagonist and helper
- Two teenagers preparing for an exam.
- Getting ready for prom night.
- Two friends driving across Scotland.
- A master and a servant.
- People trying to quit gambling.

Protagonist and two helpers (one supportive and one skeptical)
- Three friends breaking into a deserted house.
- Three sportspeople in training.
- Three convicts planning a prison break.
- Three advertising executives creating slogans for new products.
- Three singers dreaming of showbusiness.

Protagonist and a threshold guardian
- Someone trying to get into a nightclub.
- Someone without enough money for cigarettes.
- An under-eighteen trying to buy alcohol.
- Someone trying to get the phone number of someone they like via a third party.
- A gamer confronting an online challenge.

Resistance, bridging and obstruction lie at the very heart of these scenes.

Protagonist and nemesis

- An art teacher needs permission from the deputy headteacher for new supplies.

- A builder turns up to do a job only to find their rival there already.

- A sheriff finally meets the outlaw who killed their family.

- Dog owners at a Crufts-style competition.

- Two estranged siblings meet up again at a family reunion.

In each of these scenarios you must discover who the protagonist is and what their struggle is. You can cast roles before you start or simply begin the scenario and discover who is playing which role. They can all be played as single scenes, or the relationship can be played out across three-scene stories, five-scene stories, or any variant you choose.

Some Other Terms Employed in Storytelling

Catalysts/inciting incidents

This is the moment when the status quo will change for the first time, when the world becomes unbalanced for the protagonist. Something is going to *change*. Luke Skywalker doesn't realise he must become a Jedi until his home is destroyed and his guardians are murdered by the Empire – now he has no choice but to join the rebels. Elle Woods had no thoughts about going to Harvard to study law until her boyfriend broke off their relationship – now she will pursue him all the way there. Sometimes the catalyst appears very early on – the opening moments of *Ex Machina* see the protagonist winning a competition that will send him on a life-changing journey.

Peripeteia

Or 'turn of the wheel' – a reversal of fortune or twist of fate…
'As luck would have it.'

It can lead to horror and tragedy or it can lead to harmony
and success, hence it can be used in both comedy and tragedy.

Ideally, the seed for this twist of fate will somehow already
have been planted – Romeo cannot get his message to Friar
Laurence because of an unexpected outbreak of plague. Or,
for a more humorous example, consider reincorporation of
'The Claw' in *Toy Story 3*.

Bringing It All Together

Revisit the three- and five-scene stories and bring your
understanding of archetypes and basic story terminology to
these exercises. For example, in three chapters:

- *Chapter One* – Establish a status quo and a protagonist
  who wants something but cannot immediately have it.
  They turn down a chance to move closer to their goal
  until eventually they are propelled on an adventure.
  Note that the protagonist often has a selfish desire or
  want.

- *Chapter Two* – They go on all sorts of journeys, ups
  and downs, encounter antagonists and threshold
  guardians. Things go well – and then things go very
  badly. All is lost.

- *Chapter Three* – A twist of fate, and the protagonist
  manages to turn things around at the last minute.
  Enemies are defeated, order is restored, and the
  protagonist, having learned something, gives up their
  selfish goal for a greater good.

We can apply this to the film *Willy Wonka & the Chocolate Factory*, based on Roald Dahl's book *Charlie and the Chocolate Factory*:

One – Charlie Bucket (protagonist) lives in poverty with his large family in a very crowded house. Charlie is closest to Grandpa Joe (sidekick/helper). He dreams of the kinds of things one might experience at the Chocolate Factory, but knows he'll never win a coveted golden ticket to go there because he never has any money to buy chocolate. Until one day... Charlie finds a coin in the snow and uses it to buy a Wonka bar, and in so doing finds one of the five golden tickets permitting entry to the factory (catalyst/inciting incident).

Two – Charlie and Grandpa Joe go to the Chocolate Factory, where they meet the other ticket winners who are, in the main, selfish, spoiled and in contrast to Charlie. Wonka himself is, of course, a legendary trickster and nobody is assured of their safety. The factory workers (Oompa-Loompas) are also trickster-types. In fact, the whole factory is itself a kind of trickster character, full of lures and traps. A sinister antagonist offers rewards to the children if they agree to smuggle certain trade secrets out of the factory.

Charlie watches as greed gets the better of his companions (high points and low points) until they are eliminated one by one.

Three – Charlie, having transgressed and broken one of the rules earlier, is about to be thrown out of the factory (his lowest moment) but returns a secret gobstopper to Willy Wonka (a noble refusal to sell Mr Wonka's secrets to the enemy). A delighted Wonka reveals (peripeteia) that the entreaties of the antagonist were actually a test. Having proved himself to be pure-hearted and loyal, Charlie is finally entrusted with ownership of the factory (the greater good).

You can see that not a huge amount of plot is needed to tell this story. Having established the status quo and the values of our hero's world (honesty, decency, poverty), the catalyst is something that drives him into a very contrasting world (greed, indulgence, magic, danger). The characters experience fun and games as they go on adventures, and Charlie makes some mistakes along the way, learning as he does so, until eventually the trickster reveals his greatest trick – the whole thing has been a test and Charlie, having passed, will be rewarded.

Further Thoughts on Story

I once spent a blissful few hours walking with giraffes in Kenya. As soon as I reached out to try to touch one of them, it ran away.

Narrative improvisation can feel as delicate as this. One clumsy move and the story-giraffes start bolting. Trying to compel the story to go in a certain direction, or forcing a particular idea, seldom works. In the early part of this book we looked at the idea of channelling a moment rather than making something happen. It is the same at the level of *scene* and the same again at the level of *story*.

Of course, there are tools from the improviser's toolkit that can be used to repair a scene or put a scene back on track when it seems to be falling apart. The same is true of story. Players can make offers and suggestions that can help steer a story back in a satisfying direction, but this is usually done with experience and a deft touch. An image used in meditation likens attention to one's mantra to being as delicate as moving a floating crystal vase with a feather. Furrowing your brow to focus on your mantra – to concentrate, to force, compel or insist – will only create tension.

Effective improvised narrative work sees the players relating to each other in the moment, discovering their scenes, discovering who they are and what matters to them, but at the same time using their overall understanding of story to navigate – ideally with the gentle touch of a feather guiding a floating crystal vase.

People and relationships undergoing change is the bedrock of story. The tense improviser, experiencing storytelling as a pressure, misses what is unfolding around them. Don't scare the giraffes.

Getting into trouble early

In the same way that starting a scene in crisis can make the subsequent scene-build more difficult, opening a story with an emergency comes with similar challenges. Of course, many stories do open with crisis or emergency, and when improvising in such cases players will have to maintain the discipline of building their platforms under duress, or finding time and space after the initial crisis to create the foundation of the story.

Shakespeare's *The Tempest* opens with a storm and a shipwreck (Act One, Scene One), but what quickly follows is a calmer scene (Act One, Scene Two), in which Prospero explains the status quo to his daughter Miranda.

Kafka's *Metamorphosis* opens with an immediate emergency – the protagonist, Gregor Samsa, has woken up to discover he's been transformed into a dung beetle – and no status quo.

In the early part of a story we want to establish routine. What is the day-to-day life of our protagonist(s)? What are the values of this world? If the opening scene or scenes show our protagonist in crisis, then *being in crisis* might become their status quo.

Examples of this might be:

1. A warship constantly under fire.

2. An actor who can never remember their lines.

3. A stockbroker constantly making and losing vast sums of money under the high pressure of the exchange floor.

In each of these examples, the emergency or crisis can be the status quo, and some kind of catalyst will be required to initiate change for the environment or the protagonist. So, in the above examples:

1. The warship's crew is captured by the enemy.

2. The actor is fired and must seek new employment.

3. The stockbroker suddenly makes a life-changing gain or loss.

There aren't many examples of stories that maintain relentless, high-intensity crisis throughout. Even *Mad Max: Fury Road* has occasional pauses for breath.

Pace

Every milieu has its natural pace. The Australian outback is heavy, hot and slow (until the thunderous convoy of *Mad Max* races across it). Paddington Station implies high tempo and bustle. A summer riverboat is warm and languid.

The setting of your story will dictate its ambient tempo, but the players/storytellers must have an understanding of how and when to vary pace.

Pace is not how fast you speak, it's the speed of the emotional drive at any given moment. Cutting the correct wire to defuse a bomb may involve long, drawn-out activity with minimal movement, but the emotional pace is rapid because so much is at stake. *The Hurt Locker*, about a US bomb-disposal unit in Iraq, plays with this concept, as Jeremy Renner's character lives at a completely different pace to those around him. An addiction to danger means he abandons caution in ways his colleagues cannot comprehend. Driving your protagonists to high points or low moments requires an understanding of pace because emotions must intensify in order to build peaks or troughs.

Shakespeare opens *The Tempest* with the thrilling intensity of a shipwreck, but knows he cannot sustain that pace indefinitely. The pace changes in the following scene, as Prospero literally calms his daughter down and helps to allay her fears, reducing the overall emotional tempo.

Pace is intrinsically linked to the emotional intensity experienced by the characters. A chase scene doesn't have pace unless what's at stake really matters. Children playing tag may be moving around quickly, but the pace of such a sequence is usually slow.

In our Max and Chandra story (pages 175–7) we can see that the middle scene (where Chandra attempts to persuade Max that they should cancel their out-of-control party) is likely to have the fastest pace. Their emotions are at their highest, they are in conflict, and things are at stake that truly matter to them both.

Improvisers become insensitive to the needs of pace when they have disconnected from the story, most frequently to figure out plot. You can see players retreat into their thinking spaces. They stop engaging with what is going on around them, absenting themselves from the moment in order to become writers trying to design a story, rather than players experiencing a story from within.

Mood and tone

We have already looked at how scenes and settings suggest mood and tone, and while a story might have an overall mood, it will require contrasting dynamics from scene to scene, just as pace will require variation.

If a story is set in a haunted house, you won't want the first five scenes all to be slow, sinister and creepy. Many such stories begin a long way from the horror and allow the scary stuff to seep in slowly. Experiment with the build-up and release of suspense and tension.

Even the most niche of genres or specific settings will allow for lots of variation and contrast.

Watching and waiting

In many narrative and longform presentations the actors stand at the side or in a backline when they are not in the action. Whether they are visibly watching or observing from the wings, the players are inevitably thinking about the story, asking themselves: 'What's needed now?', 'How can I help?', 'What should I do?'

As soon as an actor begins to plan ahead they risk losing focus on what is actually happening in the moment. It's not that you can't plan ahead. Sometimes it's almost impossible not to. The mind receives a stimulus and off it goes, imagining, dreaming and creating. But as is said in meditation – 'innocently favour the mantra'. Observe the action on stage and note what is happening. Trust that your unconscious is already working on the story and your brain, when needed, will come up with all sorts of ideas.

I used to watch from the wings and my mind would race through dozens of possibilities. I would start to come up with ideas for good endings or great plot twists. Nowadays I try to let all that happen while 'innocently favouring the mantra'. I simply observe the scene that is happening, and a monologue like this might run through my mind:

> Okay. He seems happy to see her but she didn't
> seem happy to see him.

> Looks like they are putting up a marquee in a big field. I'm not sure what the occasion is yet.
>
> His name is Kamal. She doesn't have a name yet.
>
> Oh – he just called her Greta.
>
> She is still being a bit evasive. I wonder why?
>
> Their mutual friend from school – Rogan – is getting married tomorrow and that's what the marquee is for. Okay, so it is a marquee.
>
> Kamal is becoming increasingly awkward around Greta. It looks like he is attracted to her.

And so on. I'm not planning what to do next, I am simply being present with what is unfolding. Notice once again that my observation of their behaviour is often *more* important than what is actually being said.

When *Showstopper!* plays on tour or in the West End, it is presented as a two-act show with an interval. Many people assume we use the interval to plan what is going to happen in Act Two, but this isn't the case. Instead we use the interval to check in and make sure we are all aware of what has happened so far. We remind ourselves only of that which has been established. And that's it. We never plan ahead or fix anything at all. In fact, it's much more difficult to improvise around numerous preset events that must be contrived into a narrative.

We might also ask ourselves: 'What is this story about?' or 'What does the action of the first half tell us so far?' Not: 'What are we going to do next?' or 'How is it going to end?' It's good to check in with each other, and our thoughts and feelings are usually congruent. In shows without an interval we aren't able to have that discussion, but we are nevertheless still committed to discovering the theme and meaning of the story, just as much as we are interested in discovering the characters, form and genre. Stories are about something, though exactly what is often cause for debate. People will still argue as to what *Hamlet* is about for years to come, and the meaning of any one story will change as societies evolve.

What to show and what not to show

If we have watched A and B carry out a complex heist, we don't need to hear them over a coffee in the following scene explaining to their friend C all the details of what they just did. C can assume knowledge of it, or the scene can begin with them just finishing telling C the story. The audience doesn't need to see something twice unless there is something interesting or revelatory about the second telling. For example, the truth of the heist we watched in Scene One could be very different from the story A and B are telling their boss, C, in Scene Two – a case of unreliable narration.

In the same way, to have a character describe events at the same time as they are being shown is effective only if there is an entertaining discrepancy between the two. Characters can bend or distort truth in narration or reported speech.

As pace gathers in the dramatic action, we don't need to stop and explain something to a character if the audience already knows it or has seen it. If I need to keep up momentum in a narrative and a fellow improviser says: 'Hang on, what happened?' I'll rush off stage with them, saying: 'I'll tell you on the way!' rather than waste time explaining something that the audience already knows.

Furthermore, we would often rather see an event than hear characters talking about it, hence the old writers' maxim 'Show, don't tell.' A certain amount of anticipation or set-up can be fine, but be aware of bridging or delaying in storytelling.

Resistance and negation

Macbeth initially resists killing the King, but ultimately relents, after which the story moves forward.

For him not to resist at all would make him less humane and would distance us from him. It is important that we identify with Macbeth for the tragedy to be effective. The duration of the resistance is perfectly judged to achieve this.

There is no law or rule to say when a character should resist or for how long. Protagonists often resist 'the call to adventure' but are eventually propelled on their journey, out of the status quo and into the unknown. Hamlet swears revenge on the man who killed his father, but it is a long time before he enacts that revenge, and he resists his first real opportunity to kill Claudius (Act Three, Scene Three).

In *The Tall Guy* Jeff Goldblum's character is infatuated with Emma Thompson's nurse and, despite a fear of needles, continues to visit her for a course of injections simply so that he may see her. He quickly overcomes his resistance because the reward is so great, and what we enjoy instead is his suffering. Continued resistance would be significantly less entertaining.

Once resistance is introduced into a story, the company faces a collective challenge – what is the most satisfying duration of this resistance? Shakespeare's *Much Ado About Nothing* sees Beatrice and Benedick resisting their feelings for each other for most of the play, only admitting to them towards the end.

Negation is more problematic.

If, in Scene One, we learn that Dev and Priti can't get together because they are far too shy to talk to each other, it will be disconcerting to learn, in Scene Two, that they are suddenly a happy couple now. The audience will, quite rightly, think: 'Well, then why were we shown Scene One?' If the premise of Scene One – they are too shy to declare their love – is immediately negated, why did we spend time with it?

In improvised storytelling, performers often negate what has just happened because they think it is an interesting twist on the story or because they don't yet know how to further an idea.

Think about the game *'What Happens Next?'* (page 66) – we are looking to develop ideas, not negate them.

If Dev and Priti are too shy to talk to each other, despite clearly being attracted to each other, then this is the premise we want to put heat under. We might *investigate* the shyness through scenes with helpers and sidekicks: What happened to make them so shy? Have they been hurt in the past? Are they simply young and naive? We might *exploit* the shyness by having an antagonist or a trickster starts to make moves on one of them. We might put them in increasingly awkward situations to *intensify* their shyness (talking in public, mocked by their friends or community, etc.).

But what if we just negated it?

Once something happens, you can't pretend it didn't happen. It authentically *is*. There is no going back. If Dev and Priti got together, we can't pretend that didn't happen or we would be negating that as well. So we work with it. We allow it to become part of our story and we address the difficulties that arise from it. Again, there is no single answer and there are many possible ways to work with this negation. Here are some examples:

Scene One establishes that Dev and Priti are in love with each other, but too shy to broach the subject or make approaches to each other.

Scene Two establishes that they are now together and happily in love.

One option might be that all the other scenes happen in flashback *between Scenes One and Two* and the whole story is about how they got together despite their shyness. In other words, the first two scenes show us the beginning and the end of the story, and the rest of the narrative fills in that gap.

Or Priti reveals that she cast a spell on Dev to make him conquer his shyness and make his move. And it clearly worked! The use of magic here also takes us into a distinctive *genre*. But now Dev is a different, confident man, not the sweet, shy man with whom she fell in love. Will she tell him what she did? Will she reverse the spell? Will she risk losing him to give him back his autonomy?

Or Dev is devious. He later confesses to a confidante that he was pretending to be shy because he knew Priti liked men to be as shy as her. But will he reveal his deception? What happens when his friends from out of town come along and expect to see the outgoing, confident Dev that they all know so well?

I am sure you can think of many other alternatives too.

Practice will help remove unnecessary or unhelpful negations, but if they occur it's important to work with them, just as you would in a scene.

Deliberate Negation

Play scenes and stories in which actors make choices to deliberately negate a piece of action, idea or story beat. The practice of choosing to do that which you seek to avoid can be empowering, especially for players who do not realise that they are habitually negating.

It is also good practice for the rest of the group to work with negations (see 'Fiery Joe', from page 171).

Reasons why players will negate narrative beats

- Control.

- Dominating or avoiding dominance.

- Lack of listening.

- Misunderstanding of how to develop story.

- Lack of experience/confidence in furthering or advancing.

- Not knowing how to work with the idea and therefore attempting to reverse it.

- Thinking it is dramatically interesting.

- Mistaking resistance for bridging and thinking it would be better to 'get on with it'.

Repetition

I've played over a thousand narrative shows, usually with settings provided by the audience. As a result, repetition is inevitable. I have improvised dozens of musicals set in fast-food outlets and countless ghost stories set in run-down boarding houses.

Chess masters study and memorise as many games as possible. Their matches frequently begin with familiar moves and sequences, until something changes and the game opens up into uniqueness. It is the same with improvising story. There's no need to fear cliché or repetition because you will soon discover what makes the story unique. In *Showstopper!* training we would sometimes run three musicals in a row, all with the same setting, all starting in the same way, trusting that each story will blossom into something different over time.

The same applies to the characters you play. You might play hundreds of sidekicks, but each one can be fresh and new.

Other Story Devices and Techniques

Multiple timelines

The Godfather Part II is both sequel and prequel in that it alternates between the story of Michael Corleone and the tale of his father, Vito Corleone, arriving in New York years earlier.

Many plays and films play fast and loose with time. Act One of Caryl Churchill's *Cloud Nine* is set in Victorian Africa, while Act Two is set in the present day, although only twenty-five years have passed for the characters.

How you switch between these multiple stories is entirely up for discovery. It may be that one story is more prominent than the other(s), or equal weight and time is given to them all. The question is, how do these stories relate, and why is the story better for being told in multiple strands? Remember also that, with each strand of narrative added, the amount of time you can spend exploring them diminishes (unless you have the luxury of a fifty-hour improvathon…).

Alternative timelines

Frank Capra's *It's a Wonderful Life* is one of the great examples of a 'What if…?' story. Our hero is given another chance to look back over his life and see the realities and events that might have occurred. The film *Sliding Doors* and the musical *Our House* both follow a single story up to a decision point then split to follow both versions of that decision.

Narrators

Experiment with a character who can talk to the audience, like Salieri in the play *Amadeus* or Alfie in the film *Alfie*. The narrator can introduce and comment on action and characters. There could be a number of narrators, all of whom remember the story from a different perspective. The narrator may have misremembered the events they are recounting, thereby becoming an *unreliable* narrator. Narrators open up new storytelling possibilities. Enjoy the liveness of the audience connection. And don't forget that you can talk to, and develop relationships with, specific individuals. The audience does not always have to be addressed as one mass.

How much you break the fourth wall and talk to the audience is up to you, and an understanding of patterns will help you to pace your way through a narrative. For example, it's strange, and usually ineffective, when a narrator first starts speaking to the audience late on in the story. It's also unsatisfying if the narrator speaks to the audience early on and then doesn't address them again. Narrative address is often done at regular intervals, reflecting on key dramatic moments.

For some reason film noir is a genre often requested by audiences in shortform improv. The classic Raymond Chandleresque noir benefits from the leading character being the narrator as well. Any character can narrate, and you can enjoy endless options and combinations of how narrators can work.

Focus and Staging

I know improv teachers who work with the old techniques of magicians and mentalists. Students are asked to prepare a magic trick of some kind and show it to the class. It's a fiercely effective training in understanding how to lead an audience's focus and direct or misdirect their attention as necessary.

Where is the focus?

Presenting shortform comedy in a bar or on a small stage may not demand much from you in the way of stagecraft, but if you are improvising a play or narrative longform, you are going to have to be theatrically aware.

Staging

The Numbers

Working with Ken Campbell gave me a new understanding of stage dynamic and performance. One of my most enlightening sessions with him was spent on 'The Numbers'.

Below is a grid showing status in relationship to the audience, watching end-on as in a proscenium-arch theatre, with 1 as the highest-status position going down to 9 as the lowest.

UPSTAGE

⑧	⑦	⑨
⑤	②	⑥
③	①	④

STAGE RIGHT (left side) · STAGE LEFT (right side)

DOWNSTAGE

Number 1 (downstage-centre) is the highest-status position, whereas number 9 (upstage-left) is the lowest-status position.

Number 3 is regarded as higher status than number 4 because, in most Western cultures, we read left to right. For those who read right to left, numbers 3 and 4, 5 and 6, and 8 and 9 should be switched. I have had this confirmed by improvisers from Israel.

One of the highest-status entrances you can make is from the number 7 square. It's central, overlooking the whole space, and others on stage will have to turn upstage to see you.

Spend some time moving around the squares in front of an audience and note how you feel in different places. Move from square number 7 through number 2, right downstage to number 1, and you will feel a rush of empowerment within your body. Stand in number 9 and you will feel distanced and out of place.

In addition, Ken described *Five Positions of Facing* as follows:

1. Directly facing the audience.
2. Facing downstage-left or downstage-right (diagonally to the corners).
3. Facing right or left (in profile to the audience).
4. Facing directly upstage (back to the audience).
5. Facing upstage-left or upstage-right, diagonally away from the audience to the corners.

And *Five Positions of Elevation* as follows:

1. Standing on something.
2. Standing at ground/floor level.
3. Sitting on something.
4. Kneeling, crouching.
5. Lying down.

Play a game in pairs in which you give your partner three sets of three numbers. For example:

- 7–1–3 (upstage-centre, facing the audience, seated).
- 9–4–4 (upstage-left, back to the audience, kneeling or crouching).
- 2–2–1 (centre-stage, facing downstage-left or downstage-right, standing on something).

These correspond to three positions on the stage. Quickly commit the positions to memory and then play a scene in which you can only move through those positions. Move first – justify later! And as in the game *Three Unrelated Things/Five Unrelated Things* (page 109), you have to be very specific about why these moves are happening. Why exactly are you in the position you are in? And why in that part of the stage? Could this moment happen anywhere else or only, specifically, with those numbers in that position?

Experimenting with the numbers certainly offers some unusual ways to open scenes and will shake you out of all sorts of habits. Take up your opening positions, observe each other, begin with the *'You Look...'* exercise (page 90), and see where it leads you.

Status is relational. It is possible to be in a high-status square but in a low-status position to someone else, for example.

Understanding The Numbers transformed how I directed plays. Whereas many other directors/designers sometimes placed furniture on the upstage wall or the edges of the set, I started to bring items to the downstage (fourth) wall instead. Now, when someone moved away from their partner – say, to fix a drink at a downstage drinks cabinet – we could clearly see both players and their faces at any given moment.

The master–servant dynamic can also be explored very differently through an understanding of The Numbers. Instinctively (perhaps traditionally), servants stand upstage of their masters, but this is less effective than being downstage of them, turning upstage to face them. If a master sits in the number 2 square and their servant dutifully stands upstage of them in square 9, the master loses status whenever they turn upstage to look at their servant, whereas when the servant is in the number 3 square, facing their master, they are maintaining a lower status.

This developed into a game called 'The Walking Gentleman', the conceit being that, in days gone by, a leading lady would employ her own 'walking gentleman' to be her assistant/servant. The walking gentleman's job was to make sure his lady's appearance on stage looked good at all times. He may only have had a few lines, but his real skill was to position himself in such a way that, whenever the lady addressed him, she was always in the best position possible, no matter how many times the stage picture altered. Many actors struggle to play a walking gentleman effectively. They get themselves stuck upstage with little concept of the overall stage picture, and certainly struggle to help their leading lady (please note, genders are, of course, interchangeable in this game).

Tableaux Experiments

Put some chairs on the set so people can sit or stand on them. Ask a group of up to ten players to make a tableau in three seconds: 'Don't think about it too much – quickly adopt different positions of sitting, standing, facing and lying.' Then look at the image and ask: 'What is the eye most drawn to?', 'Who has the lowest status?', 'Who has the highest?'

Then ask actors to make changes. For example, make one move that reduces or raises their status in the tableau.

Groups of performers may wish to imagine the stage is a flat surface on a central pin – a seesaw that goes back and forward as well as up and down. Think about balancing the stage. If too many people are stage-left, balance stage-right. An eye for symmetry is important. Let asymmetrical tableaux be a choice not an accident.

More staging principles

Because we need to observe each other, it is easy to get stuck as 'bookends' – two players facing each other on a flat line, in profile to the audience. This is usually undynamic. Having directed many plays over the years, I have come to the conclusion that characters should only face each other in this way if they are going to fight or kiss. The flat line is confrontational or intimate, and plays ineffectively unless it has those tensions in it.

Explore strong diagonal lines. Remember that activity downstage is usually more dominant than activity relegated to the upstage wall, and in this way the audience is more likely to see what is going on for all players at any one time.

A great piece of advice from *Notes on Directing* (Russell Reich) is simply this: 'Is it nice or is it nasty?'

Imagine elastic strands connecting all the players. If a moment is 'nice' it might draw you towards someone. A 'nasty' offer may repel you. The invisible threads that bind players need to have some tension in them. Bodies in space are related and tell the story more powerfully than any words. LAMDA movement teacher John Baxter observes: 'The body never lies.' We can lie with our eyes, and certainly with our words, but the body always tells a true story.

At any given moment in a play, you should be able to take a snapshot of the stage and show it to someone who hasn't been watching. That person should be able to look at the still image and make a reasonable guess as to the basic relationships between characters. 'The woman sitting down is clearly the highest-status person on the stage. The man standing downstage of her seems drawn to her, and this woman at the back appears to be completely rejected, while this man looks like he wants to be more involved with the others.'

Every physical tableau should tell a story congruent with the action of the play. Therefore, whenever there is a change in emotion or dramatic action, the stage picture should change too. I have run many classes and workshops experimenting with an ensemble, encouraging the supporting artists to serve main characters' unfolding story in this way.

There's a popular improv game called 'Sitting, Standing, Lying' in which, at any moment in a three-player scene, one person must be standing, one person must be sitting down and one person must be lying down. As soon as one person changes position, the others must adjust accordingly. If the person sitting down stands up, one of the other two must immediately sit down. The joy lies in watching the players suddenly changing their positions and subsequently discovering why the change has happened. As with so much improvisation, the physical action happens first and the intellectual understanding or justification comes retrospectively. But this game is actually a useful inspiration for staging in general. It is perfectly possible to play a scene with a group of people seated around a table, but a variety of levels – sitting, standing, leaning, crouching, perching, etc. – creates a more dynamic stage tableau. And when someone adjusts, others also adjust. The overall tableau changes following a new thought or emotion. When three of us played the Marx Brothers in a *London Improvathon*, we played 'Sitting, Standing, Lying' whenever we were on stage, which helped us to capture the manic, farcical energy of Groucho, Harpo and Chico.

On the following page is a painting called *In Tram* by Virgilio Guidi. Which figure most draws the eye?

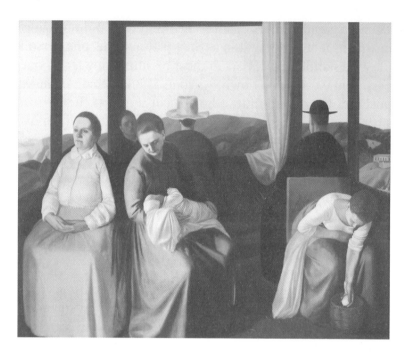

Note the two characters with their backs to us, and the woman semi-seen in the background (square 8/upstage-right).

Staging in Action

Spend some time studying and discussing the paintings and drawings of William Hogarth. Observe the many contrasting positions of facing and elevation. Also note how characters inhabit the nine squares.

Replicate these tableaux with actors in a classroom and explore the following:

- Which character or characters most draws the eye?

- Who/where is the highest-status character

- Who/where is the lowest-status character?

Ask actors to change their position in order to raise or lower their status.

Here are some of Claire Bilyard's excellent photos from the *London Fifty-Hour Improvathons*. Note the Hogarthian staging of crowd scenes using varying levels and position of facing, especially where performers position themselves downstage at a lower level, turning upstage to serve the focus of the action. In each case it is clear where the focus lies while the skillful ensemble create impressive tableaux.

Above, Justin Brett and Belinda Cornish avoid the drab 'bookends' position for two players on stage by playing diagonals and using different levels/positions.

They only move onto the flat line of confrontation or intimacy later in the scene.

And here are members of *Showstopper! The Improvised Musical* forming a tableau (including me lying on the floor!).

Mingling

The *London Fifty-Hour Improvathons* might have up to thirty performers on stage at any one time. Some shows have large casts, although even four or five players can be problematic in terms of focus if the players lack sensitivity and discipline. While many actors won't admit that they go onto a kind of 'autopilot' during long runs of rehearsed performances, it happens. Improvisers, however, can't lose attention at any point because they risk missing developments in the narrative. As a result, groups tend to gather in an arc, or curve, which, while effective for seeing everyone clearly and paying attention, looks very dull in theatrical presentation. I call this 'the arc of death'. Somehow you are going to have to break the arc, or at least use it very sparingly. Work with your group to experiment and find ways to present your show with theatrical appeal.

Here's an idea to get you started:

Play with up to sixteen players in pairs, dotted around the stage space, but have one couple occupy downstage-centre (the number 1 square) – this is designated the 'hot spot'. The focus of the scene is always here in the downstage-centre area. Players can move around as they wish, but focus is always yielded to the number 1 square. Those occupying the hot spot can leave at any time. As soon as the hot spot is left empty, another couple or group move into it and pick up the action. I'll refer to this as a *focus yield* – those who have the focus are yielding it and the new pair coming in is picking it up.

It is also possible for a couple to move downstage, in front of the hot spot, and take focus from the original pair – a *focus take*. The original players, seeing that focus has been taken from them, immediately yield the hot spot and move elsewhere.

So you can *yield* focus and you can *take* focus.

Play a scene where people mingle at any kind of social gathering, with lots of short beats between different couples and small groups, yielding and taking focus. As the scene progresses, speed up the change of focus in the hot spot.

From here you can also experiment with moving the hot spot. If, for example, a couple upstage right (in the number 8 square) suddenly burst out laughing, then the original couple yields focus immediately. The hot spot has now moved to square 8. This new couple can stay where they are – establishing a new hot spot – or can move back into the number 1 square and make that the hot spot again.

So long as everyone is listening to each other and prepared to yield or take focus, this works very well. You can get large groups of people playing complex scenes with variety in their staging, and the audience always knows where the focus is.

Part of the joy of being in a long-running company is that you can experiment with all sorts of methods of presentation, but you will find the ideas of hot spot, focus take and focus yield to be extremely helpful.

I also practise scenes with large groups using a tennis ball. Players are only allowed to speak if they are holding the ball. They can throw the ball to someone else (focus passing) or they can take the ball from the person who has it (focus taking and yielding). This mixture of passing, taking and yielding creates dynamic stage movements. There is also fun to be had with players passing the ball mid-sentence, throwing the ball to someone unexpectedly, and moving the ball around for long speeches, short exchanges and differing lengths of interaction.

Try the following settings for mingles and speaking-with-the-ball games:

- On the set of a movie.
- A science-fiction fan convention.
- Prisoners in a prison yard.
- An art gallery.
- A group of sightseers.
- A school playground.
- A camping expedition.
- A theatre company in rehearsals.

Play characters who know each other so that you can keep the game moving. As with so many pattern-based games, it should accelerate so that moving the focus speeds up as the game goes on.

Choices

Jeans and T-shirts with a beer in hand? Sharp suits? Matching outfits? You can wear whatever you like and present yourself however you wish. But remember, every small choice in a theatrical event serves the whole. Your costumes and appearance make a statement, so make it congruent with what you wish the show to be. It's the same with your choice of set and props (if any), lighting, sound design – in fact, absolutely everything from your flyers to the people who tear tickets for you is part of the concept of the show. Every choice impacts the audience. Need four chairs on the set? Which chairs? Well, what is the overall design and concept of the show? *Showstopper!* has an excellent costume design (by Gabriella Slade) with only red, white, black and grey in the colour palette (versatile colours for musical theatre), and a whole load of hats and jackets in the wings. The decision to keep these extra props and costumes concealed from the audience is deliberate. For *The Society of Strange*, players dress in faded Edwardian attire and each carries an old suitcase that can be used as a seat or a table. As the spooky tales become more modern, ties, hats and waistcoats are stripped away. The cast of *Austentatious* look extremely elegant in their Regency clothing, and their set (a simple panelled interior) is revealed from within a giant book which opens up in front of our eyes at the start of the show. *Mischief Movie Night* is played in contemporary clothing with a colour palette of blue, grey and orange. There is a single clothes rail with a few different jackets, and a two-tier stage with staircases. The feel is playful and accessible, which suits a cast playing fast, funny, movie-genre tropes.

Whether you have financial resources or not, you can agree on what the overall feel of your show is and find things within that concept. In *The School of Night* and *Rhapsodes* (in which we improvise in the Shakespearean idiom, while referencing many other dramatists along the way) we wear neutral modern clothing (dark trousers and T-shirts) with elaborate Elizabethan-style waistcoats. Our set consists only of a giant blackboard upon which we write outlines of all the challenges we will face during the show, as well as lines from Shakespeare and any other esoteric quotes of interest.

And if you feel your show is accessible shortform improv, funny and free of all these bells and whistles, then normal everyday wear is not only going to work just fine, but is perfectly in keeping with the concept of your evening.

A Short Conclusion on Story

When we looked at building scenes we observed basic principles in the face of growing complexities:

- Listen.
- Accept.
- Commit.
- Focus outwardly.
- Forward movement.

And some useful techniques:

- Endowment.
- Specificity.
- Put heat under what's there.

And some advice:

- Don't rush.
- Allow yourself to be surprised and affected.
- Innocently favour the mantra.

It is easy to get lost in the labyrinth of story. People study the subject for years. Scholars note its rich history, antecedents and cultural commonalities. It's a big subject. As with your scene work, focus on the basics:

- Keep scenes connected.
- Reincorporate ideas, motifs and themes – you don't need to know where it is going so long as you reincorporate.
- Don't be afraid to exit (it creates space in which something else can occur).
- There is no need to fear the obvious and the clichéd – surprises will *emerge*.

- Explore the story you find yourself in, not the story you feel you ought to be telling.

Remember, audiences have very little interest in watching improvisers agonise over story construction, and while they might appreciate some narrative flair they are likely to forgive scrappy moments so long as they have been entertained.

When new company members join *Showstopper!*, we give them one overriding piece of advice, more important than anything mentioned in this book so far, and it is simply this: '*Pretend you are in a musical.*'

This simple conceit usually dictates how performers in *Showstopper!* should react far more effectively than trying to remember and implement the various techniques of improv. What should I do now? Well, what would you do if you were a character in a musical? When presented with a choice about whether or not to confess his true identity in *Les Misérables*, Jean Valjean doesn't think about endowment, status or scene construction. Instead he simply sings about his agony.

Any artist has to hone their abilities with patience and study. Make sure you are working on skills that are *practical* and *practicable*. *Practical* – in that they are actually possible (some direction and coaching is impossible to put into practice and should be challenged) and *practicable* – in that they can be repeated.

My hope is that any new idea, technique, skill or practice that you come across can now be placed in a useful context – namely the principles of how scenes and stories work, and how they can be improvised.

Summary

Practise stories and scenes in three-act structure:

- The world and the premise.
- The development – going into the woods.
- The denouement – reincorporation.

Then experiment with five-act structure:

- The world and the premise.
- The development – going into the woods.
- Climax or high point.
- Low point.
- The denouement – reincorporation.

Explore stories told in linear time, and then non-sequentially with time-jumps, spins and flashbacks.

Keep scenes connected. Look to contrast scene lengths, mood, pace and tone.

Start later scenes in the middle of the action.

Develop an understanding of archetypal characters and their roles in drama.

Develop an understanding of staging, tableaux and focus. At any given moment, is the stage image congruent with the dramatic action?

Think about the concept of your show and how it affects all elements of theatrical presentation – scenic design, costumes, music, etc.

5.

Final Thoughts

To the Actor

Here's an example of my early experience with improv.

In an acting class at my dreadful drama school (a school that thankfully doesn't exist any more), I was asked to improvise a scene with a colleague. There was little guidance given as far as I recall. Perhaps we were told to play a couple.

I walked onto the stage and immediately felt very self-conscious. I had no idea where to put my attention. Within seconds my inner monologue was raging at me: 'You are being fake… This is dull.' Added to this, the actor I was working with was someone I had been romantically involved with in the past, which added to my discomfort.

My scene partner was very good (she still is) and made some bright, positive offers to try to connect us immediately.

'Hey, love – how was your day?'

'Okay,' I replied, awkwardly. 'Yeah…'

Then, slightly flirtatiously, she suggested: 'I thought we might stay in tonight. Maybe watch a DVD?' (It was the nineties.) 'I've rented *The Grifters*.' (Like I say, it was the nineties.)

I immediately responded with: 'I've already seen it.'

In attempting to compensate for my grotesque discomfort, I was negating her offers, refusing to engage or play, and preventing anything from developing.

'What's up?' she asked. 'Are you okay?'

She was being rather brilliant, playing off my mood, using what was obvious rather than pretending something wasn't happening. She was discovering what the scene was really about, a relationship in which something mattered to her character.

'What's up?'

'Leave me alone,' I said. And left the stage.

Leaving the stage was my best contribution to that scene.

I didn't look up to engage with her, or, for that matter, with anything else. My eyes were downcast. I was having a bad day.

Note that, although I was uninteresting, negative, unhelpful and resistant throughout, my scene partner moved the scene forward, worked with what she could see, made offers (without attachment to any of them), played off my reactions, and remained connected beat by beat – or sought a connection with me at least.

Why did nobody teach me how to improvise?

Improvisation, without the craft and technique that has been developed by Johnstone, Close, Spolin and many others – including some wonderful contemporary practitioners – is mostly employed in training as an opportunity for actors to indulge themselves and experience emotion. Occasionally, when something exciting happens, it feels amazing and the actor validates this as if they have 'really done some acting'. But it's not repeatable because there was no process. It was sheer chance.

I wish more acting teachers had a better understanding of performance improvisation. Until they do, you will have to study this part of your craft yourself.

I have also found that many of my students end up developing a better understanding of improvising than the directors they go on to work with. Consequently they learn to translate what a director wants into their understanding of the craft. It's rare to find a film/theatre director who really understands how improv can be effective in both development and performance.

There are various stigmas associated with improvisation. It is still sometimes seen as the poor relation to rehearsed/scripted theatre and because it is considered primarily comedy it isn't taken as seriously or regarded as being worthwhile. Film and television have embraced improvisation with greater efficacy. After all, it's easier to capture a single moment on camera than it is to repeat or rediscover it nightly on the stage. Furthermore, many writers for television and film (especially in North America, although it is gradually happening elsewhere) have studied improv with groups such as Second City, iO, Annoyance, UCB, The Groundlings and many others. Sadly, this is not without its disadvantages, and there are some who consider improv to be *only* those systems and schools. The broadening of the picture is one of the ambitions of this book.

So improvisation for the actor-in-training is often an awkward area. Wherever I teach, I try to encourage as thorough an investigation into the subject as possible, not limiting the student to comedy, or the Harold, or longform structures, but instead developing the following:

- A desire to play and a love of playfulness.
- A love of risk and danger.
- Access to being in the moment.
- Outward focus.

- Relaxation.
- Invent nothing – deny nothing.
- A love of the ensemble and of teamwork.
- Increased bravery – the ability to give anything a go.
- Overcoming (or at least not being held back by) fear of failure.
- Deeper understanding of scene and story.
- Improved listening.
- Deeper understanding of how writers work and construct scenes.
- Deeper understanding of status, rhythm, tempo, character and characterisation.
- Freedom and confidence.
- Verisimilitude.
- Clowning.
- Timing.
- Working with an audience.
- Yield.
- Commitment to process over attachment to outcome.
- An increased understanding, in theory and practice, of all of the above when going back to working with text.
- And enjoying the work rather than tormenting oneself as an artist!

The revival of interest in improvisation has seen theatre companies embracing it in ways they haven't since the heyday of *Whose Line Is It Anyway?* Some directors and producers attempt it but fail due to their lack of understanding of the craft, while others have a flair for it, knowing how to get the best results out of their team's skillset. Most notably, there seems to be a desire to recapture liveness, interaction and involvement – hence a surge of immersive theatre, and well-known actors excited about shooting projects without a script.

Be warned – improv is not a remedy for ineffective acting (the misguided director will attempt to use it as such), and one hopes you will learn to be an effective actor both on- and off-script. But experimenting with improvisation and understanding its application can make you a better actor when you return to script, and there are increasing opportunities to make a living without one.

To the Improviser

I don't want my surgeon to have 'done some workshops on medicine'.

Stanislavsky said: 'I wish the stage were a tightrope so that none but the most experienced would walk it.'

There are four years of training before you become a junior doctor, and roughly the same amount of acting training before you enter the arts as a novice.

Admittedly, at the moment there are relatively few places in the world where you can go and study improvisation with the same kind of intensity, focus and breadth of experience as an actor does at a drama school. But meanwhile, consider there are better ways to study and improve than naming the teachers you did a workshop with. Forge your own path, hone your skills and stand on the strength of your work.

'Ladies and gentlemen, this is your pilot speaking. We will shortly be taking off. Flight time estimated eight hours and twenty-five minutes. I've done six workshops on flying and one of them was with Bill Grazhny, so you're in safe hands.'

I'm not telling you not to do workshops. I'm suggesting you put things into a broader context. Your greatest qualifications will be experience and your willingness to play with others. Nobody will care about your background or training if you are a delight to play with. And remember that 'levels' are indicators of one type of training. There are many martial arts that don't have belts or ranks of any kind. There are no 'levels' in acting, and once an actor is in demand it will no longer matter where they trained, or, indeed, if they trained at all.

Work out why you are improvising. If it's a hobby – great. Enjoy it and focus on what it gives you in your life. There are many benefits:

- It can be a fun, social environment.
- Self-expression.
- Building confidence.
- Teamwork and group dynamic.
- Community and sharing.

And while you must never mistake it for therapy, it can certainly be very therapeutic.

If you want to do improv as a career, you must remember that it has a different profile in different countries. There are more opportunities to study it and work professionally at it in North America, but (IMHO) the nature of the work is much broader in Europe and the UK. The UK scene has developed significantly over the last ten years and shows no signs of slowing down, so the omens are there for bridges to be built between improvisers and theatre/TV companies.

Until that time it is likely to be tough, much like starting out as an actor, but without anything like the number of opportunities and outlets for work that actors have – and that's saying something, as any struggling actor will testify. You will need to find ways to supplement your income while improving your skills, and the chances are you will be pursuing work opportunities in other forms of acting and performance at the same time.

And remember that improv *is* acting – it simply covers the many forms of acting without scripts and lines to learn. So, if your acting is underdeveloped or you didn't train as an actor, you are going to have to work hard on those skills. Know how to use your voice and body as any actor would; learn about stagecraft and the dynamics of different spaces; investigate the numerous approaches to acting, from Stanislavsky to Strasberg, and find which ones you like and which work for you; learn how to engage with audiences; and explore everything. You will find some subjects have direct and obvious correlations with improv, such as clowning and mask.

With luck you will have opportunities to travel with the work. There are many improv festivals all over the world with a real community spirit about them (the ones I've played anyway). It's not uncommon to turn up in a new city and have the improvisers house you, feed you and show you around. In the main, improvisers are smart, playful, community-minded folk who want to encourage the best out of each other. To date, improv has taken me to twelve countries and well over three hundred theatres. It can be quite an adventure.

To the Teacher

If you are a teacher of improvisation, I implore you to consider the following:

You must *do* some improv. This is not a theoretical subject. You don't need to be good at doing it to teach it, but you do need an understanding of its complexities from the inside, if only to pay attention to your inner monologue while playing, which for me is one of the most challenging aspects of teaching and learning this subject. I am constantly checking in on thought processes, watching a scene and then finding out what people were saying to themselves while the scene was going on. A new cast member of *Showstopper!* said: 'I can play the scene okay but in my head I am going "Aaaaarrrrrrgghhh!" Is that natural?' He soon found out that he was not alone in experiencing panic while improvising. I encourage you to tune into the difficulties you experience when performing improv.

Understand that there are many different ways to improvise. There is no problem with specialising in one area if you so choose, but never be so crass as to say *your* way is the only way or the best way. Allow and encourage your students to explore all the options – improv comedy UCB-style, or Second City style, or Johnstonian scene work, or *Commedia*, or clown, or… anything. I am optimistic that one day there will be a school of improvisation akin to a drama school where students can train in the numerous disciplines available and not be at the mercy of a disparate workshop system.

In the same way I believe the improviser often reveals their subconscious state during a scene (and I therefore coach performers to listen to what they are saying), *listen to what you are saying as a teacher*. If you find you are always saying the same thing, then it may be a piece of direction for *you*, not the performers. I repeatedly told the students of one class that their tense concern about 'getting story correct' was lessening their immediacy and playfulness on stage. I continued to prioritise this point until I realised that I was, in fact, describing issues with my own process as an improviser.

In *Song of Spider-Man*, Glen Berger, bookwriter for the *Spider-Man: Turn Off the Dark* musical, documents his experiences on that troubled production, describing the project not so much as a Broadway show but instead as a 'machine which teaches humility'. I find this to be an extremely apposite description of improvisation.

You are part of a community (as a teacher, a leader of a community) in which the players will be vulnerable because they are using themselves as material. They will be exposed and often feel foolish. Their best and worst traits may be revealed with startling clarity. Your role is to contain, nurture, inspire and steer – not to bully or self-aggrandise.

Understand that people develop at different speeds, and some people simply might not be at a stage of their life when a particular lesson can fully sink in.

You will have to balance the progress of the group as a whole with the progress of individuals. And you will have to deal with constantly changing sociological and political influences, which are inevitably inseparable from the work. It's one hell of an adventure. But if you listen to your students, and if you are prepared to learn from them and not pretend you always have the answer; if you can say 'I don't know' when you don't know; if you can explore things collectively – to nurture each player with a commitment to their development (yes, with tough coaching when required) – then you will have the privilege of being part of someone's personal and professional development. And never forget that it is a privilege. Teaching at LAMDA has been one of the greatest joys and privileges of my life.

You are not there to tell people what you do. You are there to help facilitate what *they* might do.

'It is a poor teacher who is not surpassed by their students,' said Plato.

To the Group

Being part of a good improv troupe in which everyone loves the work and gets along is a true joy, and I sincerely hope you get to experience it. You may even find yourself involved in a few different groups – it's always good to play with new people.

Some companies have their own playing style and it would be wise to know about it before joining. In the main, people want you to be yourself and bring the skillset that is uniquely yours.

Be respectful. Turn up on time. Try not to bring your baggage into the room. Don't obsess over feedback and don't inflict your tension on others. You are all in it together. Support other people and they will support you.

Cultivate a love of hard work. You'll have more fun that way. Making fun the primary objective is usually counterproductive and, to be honest, a little infantile. Musicians work on their scales and arpeggios for years before they play with freedom and fluidity, and no decent athlete expects to perform well without hours of training. Sometimes training is enjoyable, sometimes it isn't, but a commitment to it will bring you closer to achieving the real joys available to you in improv.

If it's your group, make sure the environment is manageable. Allow everyone to communicate openly and freely, but let it be clear who is in charge (even if that role rotates within the group). Leadership is important.

Don't obsess over formats and structures. Above all, don't copy other groups. Find your own ways of doing things, of presenting yourselves – how you look, what you wear, how you use the stage. Learning tags and sweep edits is only useful when you are playing with those who have no other methods of interaction (it's a universal shorthand). But if you have a group that works together regularly, find your own vocabulary of movement and communication. You might come up with ideas that everyone else suddenly wants to copy.

If you want to do something that you see another group is doing – ask them. I import Die-Nasty's *Soap-a-thon* (renamed the *London Fifty-Hour Improvathon*) from Canada with permission from its originators, and they are fully credited on all marketing associated with the event. I make sure people new to the event know its origins, and I make certain the Die-Nasty players know they are welcome to join. It's a common decency often lacking among improvisers. So… credit your sources where possible and seek originality in your work.

The Harold is one way of doing things. Explore formats, learn from them, and then move on. Scrap the horrendous longform backlines unless you find a way of making them integral to the work. Think about your presentation. Think about how you communicate with your audience. Aspire. Dream big.

Working with an audience is essential and you can only be in the rehearsal room for so long, but without a certain skillset (or naive charm and flair) it is challenging to perform in front of a crowd. I suggest you don't set any fixed value on your initial performances by adopting the 'pay what you want' approach, asking the audience to pay whatever they think the show was worth in a bucket collection at the end. It gives you licence to experiment, mess up, and play freely. Once you set your price at £25–50 per show, you have to be consistently able to deliver entertainment worth the price of admission.

As an audience member who has watched a great deal of improv, I can tell you it's insulting to be told afterwards: 'Bit of an off one tonight, we were trying a new format and don't know it very well.' If that's the case, don't ask your audience for money. Or better still, tell them it's an experimental night in advance. You will find that many audiences love watching new and developing work, but they would rather know that was the case before they buy a ticket.

When Dylan Emery and I started *Showstopper!* there were only a handful of groups that held regular rehearsals. I remember being openly mocked for rehearsing. Ultimately, it all depends what you want to do. If you have twenty years of improv comedy experience under your belt, you are very unlikely to need to meet up with your regular group on a comedy night and rehearse. But if you are developing a theatrical endeavour with a different set of aspirations, you'll need to put in the hours *collectively*.

I recommend playing shortform in front of paying audiences for a while before you embark upon more ambitious storytelling projects. You will probably acquire both good and bad habits from this exercise, but you will get used to working your craft in front of a crowd and learn how to listen to your audience as much as your fellow players. Take turns sitting out of your group and watch them perform instead. What is the audience's experience of your show? What can you learn from audience reaction?

And Finally…

I can honestly say that some of the most enjoyable moments of my life have been directing improvisation in a theatre. On occasion I have laughed so hard I thought I would be hospitalised. I have been so startled by the sheer bravery and beauty of the performers with whom I am fortunate enough to work that I have often been moved to tears. On occasion, traditional theatre has affected me as profoundly, but there is something deeply magical about the wonder of spontaneous performance, where community, spirituality and a damn good time all dance together. When I recall my favourite memories of theatre, most of them were improvised.

Physicists are trying to distill the essence of the universe into one unifying theory, a desire to tie all strands of complexity into one fundamental principle, a 'This Is It' of our existence. And performing in theatre, be it on- or off-script, also aspires to find its oneness. Just be there. Be in the moment. Be a channel for what is happening right now. Let the moment play you.

I once walked into a classroom at LAMDA to find the stage area bare except for two chairs lying on their sides. I asked the group to improvise a scene inspired by this. Two actors stepped into the playing area and began a scene about two artists studying a piece of abstract art. It was a pretty dreadful scene. The more they talked, the more they started to speak purely from their subconscious, revealing their insecurities and vulnerabilities about themselves and about art itself:

A. I don't know what to do.

B. Well, we have to do something.

A. We need to make art.

B. Is this art?

They were, without conscious awareness, commenting on the fundamental challenges faced by the improviser walking onto a stage:

– What do I do?

– I have to do something.

– Is this art?

The minute you get up into the playing area *something is already happening.* The real question is, will you let it affect you? Or will you use one of the numerous techniques mastered by human beings to avoid being present?

As the scene continued, the rest of the class became restless and lost focus, much in the same way the actors were. I had the feeling that a profound lesson was occurring in the room. Did these actors get up to play this scene and create it themselves, or was the scene always there and they simply happened to walk into it? Was it like the sculpture always in the block of stone? Was this scene inevitable?

Who left the chairs in those odd positions? Was it the class who were in the room before us? Why were the chairs placed so oddly? Whoever left them like that handed us an extraordinary gift, a chance for us to learn something about ourselves and experience a genuinely revelatory lesson. So I asked: 'Who left those chairs there?'

The class replied: 'We did.'

They had been practising something else prior to our session and had left the chairs overturned on the floor. By accident? Who knows?

The end is in the beginning.

The sculpture is in the block of stone.

The story is all around us.

It is happening right now.

Appendix One

Working with Audience Suggestions

Anyone who has performed shortform comedy will tell you that they have had to endure several scenes set in proctologists, gynaecologists, STI clinics, toilets and other such settings, suggested from a desire to shock or subvert. The suggestion induces a laugh from the rest of the audience, but the person making it has no concept of what the ensuing scene might look like. They simply want to get the room laughing, impress people and lay down a challenge to the improvisers. There is a power exchange inherent in the call.

You don't have to take the first suggestion you hear. It is *your* job to provide great comedy and drama, not the audience's. If the audience could play better scenes than you, they should be performing instead.

When we ask for a setting for a musical in *Showstopper!* I am occasionally shocked by what people are prepared to shout out in public. 'A serial killer's basement' has been offered (more than once), as have war zones, and other areas of terrible human suffering. On rare occasions, when we felt the majority of the audience genuinely wanted something in this area, we have taken it upon ourselves to deliver something profound and beautiful, to honour the setting. And while this may be fine when performing a musical, it's not something that a late-night comedy crowd is likely to be keen on.

Remember that people who are prepared to shout out their ideas in front of a room full of strangers will tend towards extrovertism. The introvert thinking: 'I'd love to see a scene set in Vincent van Gogh's studio' is unlikely even to raise their hand, let alone call it out.

So how you deal with suggestions depends upon what kind of show you are doing, what kind of company ethos you have, and where you are doing that particular show.

Many audience members come up with fantastic ideas and suggestions that inspire the performers to do great work. Italian troupe I Bugiardini often encourages audience members to compete for the 'classiest suggestion'. Sometimes an atmosphere must be cultivated to give the audience confidence and permission to do so.

Matt Schuurman of Canada's Rapid Fire Theatre says the company often enjoys getting an adjective from one half of the audience and a noun from the other half. These two separate elements from different sources can create unusual discoveries. Or they may simply ask: 'What do you want to see a scene about?' – which can provoke a more imaginative and inspiring response. Crude and unhelpful replies, as usual, can be judiciously ignored.

Becky Johnson of The Sufferettes says her favourite 'ask-fors' are those that steer the audience into specific personal responses. She recalls seeing an improviser once asking: 'Has anyone here read a good book lately?' with the follow-up question: 'What would you say was the *theme* of that book?' The specificity of this kind of investigation can generate a richer scene. Appearing at the London Jam in 2014, The Sufferettes performed a show based entirely on smells.

Audience members were invited on stage to smell unmarked jars with a variety of contents and then asked what memories they triggered. These unusual approaches can generate more layered impulses in the performers and make for more surprising work. Johnson further asserts that getting deeper into someone's memories and opinions heightens her respect for the material she creates.

In *Rhapsodes*, we celebrate any audience member who contributes stories or ideas, re-enforcing how crucial their sharing is to the show. We ask for their name, often work their name and character into the show, and get the rest of the audience to applaud them for their contribution.

Appendix Two

Naming Characters

Your narrative will have characters and these characters will have names.

I recommend naming people early in scenes and repeating the name a few times so that everyone has a chance to remember it. Two problems crop up repeatedly in this area.

First, when the improviser is under pressure to be funny, they create a silly joke name. While this may induce laughter in the moment, it can become very wearing to persist with it for a whole story. A jokey name can undermine a character when more serious moments are required. It all depends upon the nature of your presentation, but why not look for inspiring names as you would have in a novel, play or film? A Victorian explorer could be Wiggle Shufflebottom, but she could also be called Scarlett St James. Calling a German character Adolf Schnitzelfrump is goofy and stereotypical, when Rudy Lang might be richer and more evocative. I certainly feel more inspired when given an evocative name by a colleague. I immediately want to live up to it. Maybe it's a question of taste but for me, a classy name endures. *Lord of the Rings* would feel considerably less epic if Frodo Baggins was called Tonkerbell

Littlepoo and Aragorn was called Clumpy Swordmunch. Names can be fun and/or funny but they must also serve your story. This matters less in shortform where the narrative does not continue beyond the scene.

I have also noticed lots of characters with names like John Smith-son-sen. The improviser, having said the obvious in 'John Smith', immediately judges themself for being uninteresting and tries to improve the surname by adding to it. Smythe-berg, Smith-sonian, Smith-bottom – you name it, I've heard it – and then everyone is stuck with a character called Smith-bottom for the next hour. Simple and elegant works well for narrative improv, and remember that, ultimately, the name of the character is less interesting than what he or she does.

Showstoppers Ruth Bratt and Pippa Evans developed a naming game where players stand in a circle and quickly contribute names in response to a given occupation.

- A music-hall entertainer – Penny Parker, Mollie Morgan, Douggie Day.

- A disgraced upper-class politician – Richard Lemster, Barbara Fordham.

- A 1950s New York Mafia boss – Joey DeMarco, Frankie 'Toots' Monroe.

Or they might make up a name and everyone else would say what kind of character they thought it would be:

- Who is Sal Marivaux? Might she be a female gunslinger? A French chanteuse? A sci-fi novelist?

In *Showstopper!* we aim to name characters congruent with the setting unless we are happy to make a joke with one, confident it will not cheapen the narrative.

Second, names can get forgotten or confused and characters can be misnamed. A strangely common occurrence is for a performer to endow a character with a name they themselves have just been given, suddenly resulting in two Roberts. This is because the performer, in concentrating to remember their own name, finds they accidentally endow someone else with it. As we work with what *authentically is*, we must now continue with two Roberts.

We all find ourselves in scenes where we have missed some important endowment or piece of information, and a name can be a paralysing example.

If you are sitting at the poker table, watching your stack of chips diminishing, and you haven't been involved much in the action, there comes a point at which you have to make a stand about something. You can't let the game erode your resources and pass you by without making a contribution at some point. It's the same in a scene where you feel mis- or under-informed. Try something. Say the name you think it is. If you are right, then there is no problem. If you are wrong, something will come from that moment. If you called your lover Steve when his name was in fact Devon, it could reveal an affair, or the beginnings of a nervous breakdown. There is no such thing as a mistake. Bet big and embrace the result.

Index of Concepts and Exercises

Page numbers refer to the first introduction of a concept, principle or idea, though many are explored throughout the book in subsequent sections.

Games and exercises are indented and italicised below.

www.nickhernbooks.co.uk

facebook.com/nickhernbooks

twitter.com/nickhernbooks